Edwardian Country Life

EDWARDIAN COUNTRY LIFE
The Story of H. Avray Tipping

HELENA GERRISH

F

FRANCES LINCOLN LIMITED
PUBLISHERS

To Hilary who bought me High Glanau, with love

Frances Lincoln Limited
4 Torriano Mews
Torriano Avenue
London NW5 2RZ
www.franceslincoln.com

Edwardian Country Life: The story of Henry Avray Tipping
Copyright © Frances Lincoln Limited 2011
Text copyright © Helena Gerrish 2011
Pictures copyright © as listed on p 208

First Frances Lincoln edition 2011

A catalogue record for this book is available from the British Library.

978-0-7112-3223-5

Printed and bound in China

1 3 5 7 9 8 6 4 2

Commissioned and edited by Jane Crawley
Designed by Anne Wilson

FRONT ENDPAPERS The grassway below the south terrace at Chequers,
photographed by A.E. Henson for Tipping's *Country Life* articles in 1917.
BACK ENDPAPERS Pergola at Mounton, 1915.
PAGE 1 Henry Avray Tipping's 1908 diary.
PAGES 2–3 Grass alley and topiary at Mathern Palace in 1910.
PAGE 5 Cartoon of Tipping drawn in 1915 by Hubert D. Astley (detail of page 53).

Contents

Introduction

HENRY AVRAY TIPPING was a much respected academic, writer, collector and patron. For over forty years he had visited and accurately recorded nearly every important country house in Britain and his influential articles for *Country Life*, with their superb photographs, detailed the social, historical and architectural development of each property. He was a pioneer in the writing of finely illustrated and authoritative books on houses, gardens and furniture and became a major influence on the history of taste. In his own time he lived the life of an Edwardian country gentleman and was the centre of a network of architects, designers and wealthy patrons; yet it seems he always strove to protect his private life and on his death in November 1933 he ordered that all his personal papers should be burnt. Perhaps that is the reason his name is so little known – although anyone who does research on the architecture and gardens of the great British houses will soon come across it.

Although his character was enigmatic and his style of life relatively reclusive in his final years, Tipping had a gift for friendship. In the Oxford of Pater and Ruskin he wore his hair long, sported a hyacinth in his buttonhole and proved to be a fine actor as well as a first class historian. He had an incisive manner of speech and an unusual way of expressing himself, but he was genial, amusing, generous to his friends and, according to his colleague Ralph Edwards, 'supremely self-confident and resolutely determined to get his own way'.

His passion for plants, flowers and trees, designing gardens for himself and for others, was shared with his friends Harold Peto and George Herbert Kitchin. He discovered Iford Manor with Peto and often stayed there during the early years of that garden's evolution.

ABOVE The Tipping family crest and motto, 'Live that you may live'.

LEFT H. Avray Tipping photographed in about 1914.

ABOVE Pencil drawing by G.H. Kitchin of Munstead Wood by Ned Lutyens for Miss Gertrude Jekyll, 19 August 1901.

The architect George Herbert Kitchin, whose traditional Arts and Crafts home and garden at Compton End near Winchester was illustrated in *Country Life* in 1919, was a lifelong friend and trusted architectural adviser. He drew the sketches of buildings for many of Tipping's books, and the garden design for Compton End is the endpaper for Tipping's last publication *The Garden of To-day*. Recently discovered, Kitchin's sketchbooks form a pictorial diary of Tipping's life, from his birthplace at Ville d'Avray, his homes at Mathern Palace, Mounton House and High Glanau in Monmouthshire, right up to Harefield House in Middlesex where he died; and they give a charming insight into their joint visits to village churches and old country homes, their holidays with Jack Tremayne of Heligan and architectural jaunts to Ned Lutyens's new houses or Gertrude Jekyll's home at Munstead Wood.

Tipping's colleagues were men and women of outstanding ability in their fields. They included Gertrude Jekyll, the great gardener and plantswoman whom he called an 'entirely capable woman', William Robinson, with his highly successful gardening journals and crusade for natural planting, Christopher Hussey, the greatest architectural historian of modern times, who always called Tipping his 'mentor', Edward Hudson, the founder of *Country Life*, Lawrence Weaver, the architectural writer, and furniture experts Percy Macquoid and Margaret Jourdain.

Tipping owned a succession of three houses in Monmouthshire. First he restored the ruined Mathern Palace, the old medieval palace of the Bishops of Landaff, to make it 'habitable as a place of modern residence with as little serious interference as possible with its picturesque aspect and archaeological interest'. His next home was Mounton, where he built one of the last grand country houses in Wales and entertained Lloyd George and Stanley Baldwin. Finally at High Glanau, with its spectacular view towards the Brecon Beacons, he created the perfect Arts and Crafts blend of vernacular architecture and formal gardens in the setting of a wild garden, rustic pathways and a stream. He loved the

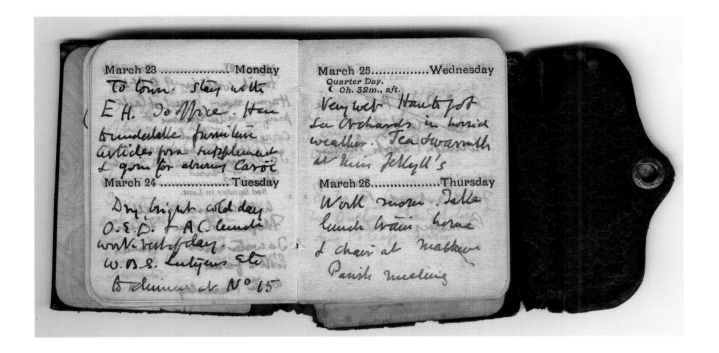

ABOVE Page of Tipping's 1908 diary, noting staying with Edward Hudson, dinner with Lutyens and tea with Gertrude Jekyll.

picturesque effect of a garden on a steep Welsh hillside, the peace and seclusion of a fernery and the sensuality of bathing in the cool waters of the pools he made in his woodland gardens. But in reality he was a restless soul, always moving on to a new challenge.

When he died Tipping was a rich man with estates in Middlesex, Oxfordshire and Monmouthshire, and he held an important collection of oak furniture, paintings, wood carving, silver and porcelain. To the public he was an educator, writing both before and after the First World War and fully aware of the permanent social shift the war brought about and its effect on country living. He was a considerable expert on political economy and a man with a social conscience, yet he left his money not for the creation of a new garden suburb, nor to the National Trust, nor to the Society for the Protection of Ancient Buildings, nor to the National Gardens Scheme which he had helped to form. Instead he left everything to a thirty-one-year-old gardener who then burnt his papers, sold his estates and quietly let his benefactor's name sink into oblivion.

Fortunately Tipping's houses, gardens and writings provide an objective testimony to his significance; and we are fortunate to have one more subjective and personal record. The Crockett family, who worked for Tipping at Mathern Palace, somehow held on to one diary which has been passed down through the generations and lent to the author. This means that in that one year of 1908 Tipping's life is fully documented, with details of his visits to country houses, sometimes twenty in one week, his dinners with Edwin Lutyens, Gertrude Jekyll, William Robinson and Lawrence Weaver at Edward Hudson's home at Queen Anne's Gate, his making of the water garden at Mounton, his visitors, his writing, his sleeping in the open air. It provides a hitherto unknown glimpse into the life of an intriguing man, a man who not only wrote about the Edwardian country life but lived it to the full.

ABOVE Ville d'Avray in an oil painting by Jean-Baptiste-Camille Corot (1796–1875).

RIGHT Tipping's birthplace, the Chateau de Ville d'Avray.

Henry Avray Tipping 1855~1933

Henry Avray Tipping was born in 1855 at the Chateau de Ville d'Avray in a village near Paris. The eighteenth-century chateau had been built by Marc-Antoine Thierry in 1776 and boasted a chapel, a concert hall (where Louis XVI attended a theatrical performance), an orangery, stables and a farm. Thierry created impressive gardens with pools and fountains in the river valley. Camille Corot's summer home was in the village and many of his paintings show the charms of Ville d'Avray. In the year Tipping was born, Corot was painting the frescoes in the local church. Tipping's parents were much attached to the culture of France; they collected French furniture and porcelain (the Sèvres factory was nearby) and lived in the chateau for two years before moving to Brasted Place in Kent.

Tipping's father, William Tipping, born in Liverpool in 1816, was the son of a prominent Lancashire corn merchant and was descended from a long line of Quaker yeomen. He was deeply interested in archaeology, sketching and painting. In his twenties he spent six years travelling in the eastern Mediterranean, making drawings of little known and inaccessible tombs in Palestine, often in perilous circumstances. Engravings of his drawings were advertised in *Punch* in 1851. His knowledge of archaeological sites led to his election to the Society of Antiquaries in 1864. Among his close friends were Lord Stanhope of nearby Chevening who was responsible for the foundation of the National Portrait Gallery and Sir John Evans, President of the Society of Antiquaries.

As squire of Brasted Place, William Tipping immediately set about improving the village, which he had found in a deplorable state, conspicuous for its poverty and insanitary dwellings. He restored dilapidated cottages, rebuilt boundary walls, widened roads and planted avenues of trees. He abhorred idleness, and local manual workers soon found that he could always find a job for them to do. He was a powerful backer of religious and educational institutions in the village and a strong supporter of social welfare and patriotic activities. His wise counsel and moral and financial support were freely given.

In 1865 William Tipping accepted an invitation from friends in Stockport, then a liberal stronghold, to stand as Conservative candidate in the parliamentary elections. He served as Member of Parliament from 1868 to 1874, but lost his seat at the 1874 election. He was re-elected in 1885 but did not defend his seat at the 1886 general election. His abiding interest in railways was formed when, as a boy, he witnessed the construction of the Liverpool and Manchester line. By 1876 he had become a director of thirteen railway companies including the London and North Western; one of his special functions was to arrange the travel of the royal family. He formed the Westerham Valley Railway Company, guaranteeing £50,000 to enable the necessary private bill to be passed by the House of Commons in July 1876. The construction of that railway began in 1876 and was completed in 1881, soon to be absorbed by the South Eastern Railway. The new line, with its stations at Dunton Green, Brasted and Westerham, was warmly welcomed by local traders and landowners. Hops were grown in the fields around Brasted and there were nurseries sending flowers, fruit and vegetables by train to London for Covent Garden market.

The squire, who was Justice of the Peace for Kent, Lancashire and West Riding, was a familiar sight in the village with his, 'tall figure, bald head and grey curls, whiskers and a Newgate frill, and square-topped hard felt hat'. On his return from the 1885 election victory, the men of Brasted unharnessed the horses from his carriage and pulled it through the village, while members of the fire brigade in their uniform formed a guard of honour and a drum and fife band led the way to the mansion. When William Tipping died on 16 January 1897 – at the age of eighty in the year of Queen Victoria's Jubilee – the village was plunged into mourning. The long funeral cortège of carriages and walkers was witnessed by hundreds of people, many of whom queued past a lying-in-state of the funeral bier to pay a last tribute. The *Westerham Herald* wrote, 'No man ever became more popular, or was more beloved by his neighbours than Mr Tipping. His loss will be severely felt throughout the district.' His passing severed one

ABOVE Tipping's father, William Tipping, MP for Stockport.
RIGHT Pencil drawing of an unidentified Damascus house with its *hawsh* (open courtyard), fountain and *takhtabush* (recessed area for sitting) drawn in Syria by William J. Tipping in 1840.

of Brasted's links with a vanished age. His resplendent barouches, broughams and landaus, with coachmen and footmen attired in scarlet and green, rumbled along sleepy country lanes where the sound of motor traffic was as yet quite unknown. His paternal influence over the well-being of the village was exerted at a time when public welfare facilities were few. He brought to Brasted material wealth from railways and industry and wise guidance during a period of perplexing social and economic change. He was laid to rest in the family vault at St Martin's Church, Brasted. In 1901 the family erected a village hall in his memory.

Tipping's mother, Maria Walker (1822–1911), also from a Quaker family, was the daughter of Benjamin Walker, a prosperous flax spinner from Leeds. William and Maria married in 1844 and both displayed characteristic Victorian individualism. They believed in helping others to help themselves and were noted for their unobtrusive good works, a family trait that their youngest son Henry Avray was to continue throughout his life. Maria was a great supporter of slum clearance schemes and also rehousing for the industrious poor and housing estates for artisans and middle classes. She left a substantial legacy to Destitute Waif Children, now known as Dr Barnardo's. After her husband died, Maria lived with her youngest son for the last fifteen years of her life, and died at Mathern Palace in Monmouthshire in December 1911.

William and Maria raised four sons. The oldest, John Walker (1845–76), attended Harrow School and read Law at Trinity College, Cambridge. He never married but settled in Saxony and is recorded as having died tragically in a shooting incident in a ruined castle near Dresden. The second son, William Fearon (1847–1911), thus became heir to Brasted Place. From 1886 to 1894 he commanded the 3rd Battalion (Militia) of the Royal

ABOVE Tipping's mother, Maria Tipping (née Walker), aged 82 in the loggia at Mathern Palace.
LEFT Harry Tipping at Mathern Palace in the same year (1904) aged 49.
RIGHT Pen and ink drawing of Brasted Place designed by Robert Adam in 1784. This drawing was added by Dr Turton to his own copy of Watts's *Seats of the Nobility and Gentry*, 1779.

Welsh Fusiliers and was given the honorary rank of colonel in 1893. Colonel Tipping never married; he was Justice of the Peace for Kent and High Sheriff of the county in 1905 and a connoisseur of old silver, porcelain and snuffboxes. He was a keen sportsman and generous supporter of local activities at Brasted, where he restored the armorial glass in the church. When he died in 1911 he left estate to the value of £271,000 to his brother Henry, but with a letter asking that his godson, Hubert Holden, should become heir to some property on Henry's death. He also requested that £2,000 should be spent on the building of almshouses with a nurse's house in Brasted, with a further endowment to maintain them. The third son, Edward Alexander (1852–71) – said to have been 'the favourite son of the parents' by H.G. Singleton, a distant cousin – died from scarlet fever after a walk in the snow while still at Westminster School.

Henry Avray, the youngest son, known as Harry to family and friends, was born in 1855 and on the death of his third brother in 1911 stood alone as the last of the Tipping family. He inherited from his parents a love of the past, a social conscience and considerable private means (augmented by the premature death of two of his brothers and by inheritance from the third). He was well over six feet tall and of striking but rather formidable appearance. This was accentuated in later years by the loss of an eye, probably through infection. He was reputed to be hot-tempered and autocratic in manner, but was generous with money, advice and encouragement, especially to those who shared his interests in architecture and gardens. He was a great supporter of cricket and built a cricket ground for local players by each of his houses. He was a dog lover and although he never cared for hunting, shooting, fishing or dancing, he much enjoyed travelling throughout France and Britain, entertaining, walking, showing visitors the local sites, and even playing bridge. In later life he became more withdrawn, staying at home and enjoying his own gardens.

The Tipping family home, Brasted Place in Kent, was built in the neo-classical style with Etruscan details by Robert Adam in 1784 for Dr Turton, physician to George III. The original Adam design included balanced side wings, but when the king proposed a visit, Turton, dreading the honour, hastily cancelled the wings, informing His Majesty that his humble dwelling was inadequate to entertain royalty. Turton became a royal

favourite and was given magnificent Chinese wallpaper for his new home and a clock from one of the turrets from the Horse Guards which was installed above the stables at Brasted. In 1839 Emperor Napoleon III, then Prince Louis Bonaparte, planned the recovery of France from his retreat at Brasted Place. He drilled imperialist recruits on the southern lawn, attended by a tame eagle, symbol of the empire. The outcome was his disastrous expedition to Boulogne in 1840 which culminated in a French prison.

In 1853 William Tipping bought Brasted Place with approximately 300 acres for £20,000. He repaired and re-equipped the house and in 1871 added a wing designed by Alfred Waterhouse in the French chateau style. New terraces, parterres and rhododendron banks were introduced to the grounds by William Tipping, changing the character from the landscape style to one which he felt, 'presented a variety of charming vistas'. These Victorian formal gardens were never admired by his son, Harry, who was to remember the garden at Brasted in his book *The Garden of To-day*,

There were shrubberies to be dug once a year in such a manner that made the growth of perennials among them difficult and out of place. There were numbers of many-shaped beds cut out of the lawn, showing bare earth for seven months of the year, and only gay in three. Even then they were not interesting. You walked rapidly round, and said it was well done. Then you had finished with them, and said that the lawn was well weeded and the gravel paths well rolled. After that another subject of conversation had to be found.

Harry's formative years were spent at Brasted in those Victorian days before the motor car when most small boys were encouraged to be seen but not heard, but one feels his upbringing may have been far from severe with his doting, enlightened and cultured parents. The house inside was dark and crowded with heavy furniture, paintings, drawings and numerous collections of porcelain and silver, but still contained some of the splendid Chinese wallpaper given to Dr Turton by George III. The golden wedding of William and Maria in July 1894 was celebrated by a

LEFT Brasted Place, with the French chateau style wing by Alfred Waterhouse added by William Tipping in 1871.
RIGHT The Victorian gardens at Brasted Place in 1912.
BELOW LEFT The library at Brasted Place in 1912.
BELOW RIGHT The drawing room at Brasted Place in 1912.

week-long festival, with bunting, church bells, military bands and firework displays on the cricket ground. There were grand parties at the mansion, illuminated in the evenings by Chinese lanterns. Tipping's early years were thus of great material wealth, but the example of his father's paternalistic relationship with the local community, perhaps combined with his Quaker background, influenced Harry's own interest in social work later in life.

Harry Tipping appears to have received his early education partly at a Middlesex private school and partly in France. In 1874 he went up to Christ Church, Oxford. This was the Oxford of Walter Pater whose theories of aestheticism, as expressed in his *Studies in the History of the Renaissance* (1873) and his philosophical novel *Marius the Epicurean* (1885), held a strong appeal for Tipping. Pater advocated the cultivation of intense receptivity to beauty and to moments of sensation in life, art, music and literature. He tutored Gerard Manley Hopkins and Oscar Wilde and it is tempting to speculate that Tipping may have been one of his students or at least attended his lectures. Pater's works focus on male beauty, friendship and love. Benjamin Jowett, John Ruskin and Matthew Arnold were also powerful influences, as well as the poetry of Keats and the writings of Darwin, Huxley, Rabelais and Flaubert. John Ruskin, whose writings much influenced the design of the Oxford Museum of Natural History, became in 1870 the first Slade Professor of Fine Art and inspired many a student in their first ardent worship of Italian art.

Lady Celia Congreve, whose stepfather was rector at Brasted, was a close friend. Harry Tipping was twenty-two and she a girl of eleven when they first met. She wrote a personal recollection of Tipping after his death, remembering him during his time at Oxford as, 'slightly bitten by the fashionable craze for aestheticism; he wore his hair long, and large flowers, such as hyacinths, in his buttonhole'. Oscar Wilde was of course well known for wearing a lily in *his* buttonhole. Wilde had rooms in Magdalen, decorated with Pre-Raphaelite paintings, engravings and blue and white porcelain. He graduated on the same day as Tipping in November 1878 and attended Ruskin's lectures on art. It is possible that Tipping shared these current artistic enthusiasms with his fellow undergraduates. He certainly distinguished himself in the university debating and thespian circles. Lady Congreve also remembered that,

LEFT Oscar Wilde, who shared a graduation ceremony with Tipping in 1878, in a photograph by Napoleon Sarony.
RIGHT Ink drawing of Plomière-les-Bains, sketched by Tipping when he was travelling in France in 1878.

He was an important member of the Oxford University Dramatic Society – and a very fine actor – he would most certainly have made a name for himself professionally if there had not been so many other things he did better than most people! He was very fond of getting up plays for village charities.

He was a living contradiction of the saying 'Jack of all trades – master of none' for he was certainly master of everything he undertook. His versatility was amazing – he was even an excellent cook!

[Tipping's recipe for sloe gin, noted down by Peto, still survives.]

Tipping took a first in Modern History in 1878 and then travelled in France for a while. He returned to Oxford until 1881 and there was an expectation among friends that he would pursue a political career but, after a short period as a university lecturer, he joined the team working under Leslie Stephen (1832–1904) and from 1891, Sidney Lee (1859–1926), to produce the *Dictionary of National Biography*. The contributors worked at the British Museum in the morning and in the afternoon in the office at 14 Waterloo Place. Tipping worked as a researcher in genealogy and wrote the contributions for the Baldock and Beaufort families.

During Tipping's time at Christ Church, Henry Liddell was Dean and Alice his fourth child, was the inspiration for *Alice's Adventures in Wonderland*, which Charles Dodgson had published in 1865 under the name Lewis Carroll. Dodgson was the mathematics tutor at Christ Church and was to go on to become a celebrated portrait photographer. George William Kitchin was Junior Censor at Christ Church, later to become Dean of Winchester, then Durham, and his children (among them George Herbert), as well as the Liddell family, were favourite photographic subjects of Carroll.

LEFT ABOVE Photograph by Lewis Carroll of George Herbert Kitchin (the defeated soldier on the floor) with his siblings enacting St George and the Dragon in 1875. Carroll took over fifty photographs of the Kitchin children between 1874 and 1878.
LEFT BELOW Compton End, the home of G.H. Kitchin.
RIGHT ABOVE The pond garden at Compton End.
RIGHT BELOW The glazed garden room, with ever open door and steps leading up to Kitchin's bedroom.

George Herbert Kitchin (1870–1951) was an architect and a lifelong friend of Tipping, though fifteen years his junior. They travelled together to France and Belgium, holidayed in Cornwall with Jack Tremayne at Heligan and Tipping used Kitchin's drawings for many of his articles and books. In the late 1890s Kitchin bought Compton End near Winchester, where he practised in the Arts and Crafts style. He restored and expanded the old farmhouse and over the next twenty years, transformed the garden with hedged enclosures, topiary (including a yew arbour similar to the one at Tipping's Mathern Palace – see page 95), new paths and a pond garden. His glazed garden room, with a view down a paved path to the wilder garden, was a favourite place of Tipping's and he wrote about it and illustrated it many times. 'Compton End is a deliciously enjoyable *multum in parvo*,' he wrote in *English Gardens*. They obviously shared a love of an outside garden room, used all year round, where one could eat with the doors flung wide open. There were outside stairs up to a terrace and bedroom and Tipping adored sleeping in the fresh air; he often designed sleeping huts, open air loggias and tea houses for his own gardens.

LEFT The Quarry, the house on the Brasted estate where Tipping made his first garden.
RIGHT The steps in the Quarry garden at Scotney Castle, home to the Hussey family who were friends of the nearby Tipping family.

After the freedom of Oxford he must have felt that living with his family was too claustrophobic and he moved to his own house on the Brasted estate, known as The Quarry. This had been built by Durtnells of Brasted and may have been to Tipping's specification. He probably entertained his friends there as it had five bedrooms, an entrance lodge, a coachhouse and stables. Here, he was studying art, architecture and furniture and developing his interests in plants and garden design and, for the first time, he made a garden. He landscaped the quarry making a picturesque rock garden with bridges and walkways, and added a tennis court and croquet lawn near to the house. The quarry was a favourite element in the Picturesque landscape garden, and Tipping may have been inspired by Payne Knight, known for his theories on picturesque landscape, who wrote in 1794,

> The quarry long neglected, and o'ergrown
> With thorns, that hang o'er mould'ring beds of stone,
> May oft the place of nat'ral rocks supply,
> And frame the verdant picture to the eye.

But Tipping's rock gardens were the result of careful thought rather than neglect. A model for this particular one may have been the quarry at Scotney Castle, the nearby mansion belonging to the Hussey family, who were great friends. Tipping wrote about the Scotney quarry in *English Homes* in 1925,

> By a very judicious arrangement of walks winding round real obstructions, but a right ordering of the broken ground so that it should look as though Nature had improved her own swells and curves, and by a free use of good material in planting, this early wild garden can well compete with the best of the later ones.

Rock gardens had become popular, with many being designed by James Backhouse, a Yorkshire nurseryman and Quaker missionary. Tipping introduced rustic bridges, stepping stones and canalised streams and added ferns, azaleas, rhododendrons and *Primula bulleyana* in several of his own grounds.

22

It was from The Quarry at Brasted that Tipping wrote his earliest printed work, a musical comedy, *A Hibernian Hyperbole, entitled the three P's, or the Pig, the Paddy and the Patriot MP*. This was a short entertainment with Tipping playing the part of the pig and music composed by A.S. Pratt (the organist at Brasted church) and it was performed at Westerham Public Hall in January 1888. The title may have been taken from Lewis Carroll's *The Vision of the three T's*, a satirical pamphlet concerning Christ Church affairs issued during the year Tipping went up to Oxford. This was directed at Dean Liddell's improvements at the college – the three T's representing the Tea-Chest (the name for the new belfry), the Trench (an 'improvement' at the southeast corner of Tom Quad) and the Tunnel (a new double arched entrance to the cathedral) and includes a song which parodied the Dean and his new building works,

Five fathoms square the Belfry frowns;
All its sides of timber made;
Painted all in greys and browns;
Nothing of it that will fade.
Christ Church may admire the change –

Oxford thinks it sad and strange.
Beauty's dead! Let's ring her knell.
Hark! Now I hear them – ding-dong, bell.

These pamphlets would have been eagerly circulated among new young undergraduates such as Harry Tipping and Oscar Wilde. The *Hyperbole* was about Irish Home Rule, and included parodies of Gladstone and Parnell. Tipping, as Widow Murphy's Pig who had the gift of speech, sang, in the style of Gilbert and Sullivan,

In the admirable leisure of a solitary sty,
I've watched the course of politics with philosophic eye
And have reached the deep conviction,
That it is purely fiction
To rank the English Radical as intellectually high.

The play is very anti politician, although it was put on to raise money for the Chevening Habitation of the Primrose

BELOW AND RIGHT Tipping's first printed work, a musical comedy performed at Westerham Public Hall in 1888.

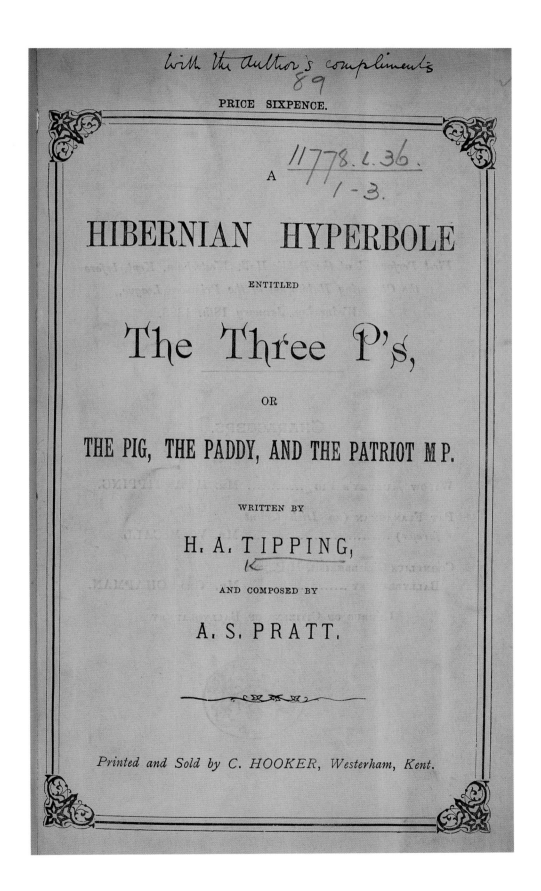

With the author's compliments

89

PRICE SIXPENCE.

11778. l. 36.
1 – 3.

A

HIBERNIAN HYPERBOLE

ENTITLED

The Three P's,

OR

THE PIG, THE PADDY, AND THE PATRIOT M P.

WRITTEN BY

H. A. TIPPING,

AND COMPOSED BY

A. S. PRATT.

Printed and Sold by C. HOOKER, Westerham, Kent.

League. One wonders what Lord Stanhope of Chevening, and his father, a Member of Parliament at that time, can have thought of it, but the latter generously paid for the local builders to make the stage sets. It corresponds with Lady Congreve's recollections of Harry, 'A man who was a great friend of his when he was about thirty told me that he knew more about political economy than anyone in England and that it would be a thousand pities he would not stand for parliament.'

In 1890 Tipping moved to Harbrook Cottage (originally known as Park Town Farm) at Ramsbury in Wiltshire. His friend Percy Macquoid, who was then a stage designer and interior decorator, was living at nearby Crowood House. The cottage was on the Ramsbury estate of Sir Francis Burdett, father of the noted nineteenth-century philanthropist Baroness Burdett-Coutts, who was known as the richest heiress in England. Whether Tipping knew Angela Burdett-Coutts is not known, but he certainly wrote the first article about Ramsbury Manor in *Country Life* in 1907. He produced two more pieces about the house in 1920. His cottage overlooked the Kennet and Avon canal and watercress beds, and the garden with its clear millstream must have appealed to him. He was later to design water gardens at each of his properties in Monmouthshire.

From the 1890s onwards Tipping bought, occupied and subsequently sold a succession of estates in Monmouthshire. It is not known why he chose this area. Richard Haslam, the architectural historian, suggests: 'The old county of Monmouthshire had one outstanding historian at the time, Octavius Morgan, who was MP for the county from 1841 to 1874'. He too had been at Christ Church, and was a fellow of the Society of Antiquaries with Tipping's father, so it is possible that Morgan and Tipping may have met before the former's death in 1888. In Monmouthshire, Tipping experimented with the ideas about which he was to write for the rest of his life. The sites were all carefully chosen, having regard to historical associations, aspect, soil, rocks and natural water. If there was no stream, he would create one – and often a waterfall – using water pumped from some distance. On these sites he restored buildings of historical importance, or erected entirely new houses to develop his ideas of design and architecture. The laying out

ABOVE Pencil sketch by G.H. Kitchin, 1894, of the interior of Tipping's cottage at Harbrook on the Ramsbury estate in Wiltshire.
RIGHT The entrance front of Mathern Palace in Monmouthshire as it appeared in an article published in 1910.

of the surroundings was a very important part of the overall design. The usual scheme was to have formal gardens close to the house and let them merge gradually into a carefully planned natural garden and woodlands.

The first of these properties was Mathern Palace which Tipping bought in 1894. He set about a serious restoration programme there and laid out romantic gardens which he wrote about for William Robinson in *The Garden* in 1900. For the rebuilding of the palace he followed the guidelines of the Society for the Protection of Ancient Buildings (SPAB), founded in 1877 to counteract the highly destructive 'restoration' of medieval buildings being practised by many Victorian architects. In 1909, following this work, he was elected a Fellow of the Society of Antiquaries. The signatories on Tipping's election certificate are significant as they show his circle of acquaintance at that time: Sir Edward Maude Thompson, who was Principal Librarian (now known as Director) of the

British Museum; William Barclay Squire (Deputy Keeper of Printed Books at the British Museum, music critic and scholar who worked there with F.W. Jekyll, nephew of Gertrude Jekyll) who was a close friend, often lunching with Tipping in London and staying with him in Monmouthshire; the Very Revd George William Kitchin, Dean of Durham, the father of Tipping's friend George Herbert Kitchin, a regular guest in Monmouthshire; Mr Everard Green, Rouge Dragon Pursuivant of Arms, who became Somerset Herald, who also stayed in Monmouthshire and was known as Dragon in Tipping's diary; Morgan Stuart Williams who was the owner of St Donat's Castle, a friend of Tipping in Wales and designer of the sundial at Buckland Hall for the Gwynne-Holford family (see page 160); Sir George Armytage, who was the owner of Kirklees Park in Yorkshire which Tipping wrote about in *Country Life* in August 1908; Lt Col. George Babington Croft Lyons, Vice-President of the Burlington Fine Arts Club; Edward

Mounton Dene, Chepstow
Oct. 13. 99 —

Hudson, founder of *Country Life*, and Lawrence Weaver, initiator of the Architectural Supplements in *Country Life*, promoting the works of Edwin Lutyens, Robert Lorimer and other Arts and Crafts architects. Tipping often worked in the Library of the Society of Antiquaries at Burlington House.

In 1905 Tipping was becoming restless at Mathern, but probably felt he could not start a new building project while his mother was still alive. So he bought a farm, Mounton Dene, and some land in the Mounton Valley about two miles from Mathern Palace and started to design an elaborate water garden. He canalised the stream for this wild garden, bringing in stone from Mathern and moving earth with a small railway. He financed these early projects with money inherited from his father. Later his income was augmented by fees

LEFT Pencil sketch by G.H. Kitchin of Mounton Dene, 1899.
ABOVE Bridge and gardener's cottage in the Mounton Valley in 1908.

charged for articles and advice given on the restoration of buildings, such as Brinsop Court in Herefordshire, Ockwells in Berkshire, North Cadbury Court in Somerset and Coombe Woodhouse at Kingston, and from royalties from his books. By this time he had started on the career that he was to have for more than twenty-eight years as a staff architectural writer for *Country Life*. His 1908 pocket diary reveals that he usually travelled to London

29

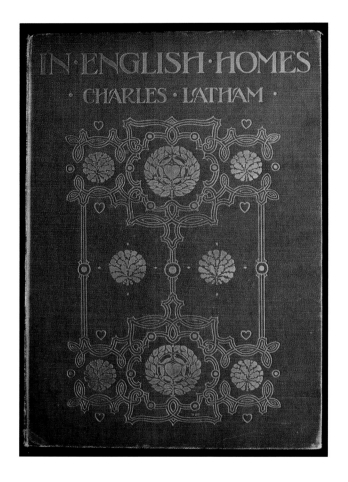

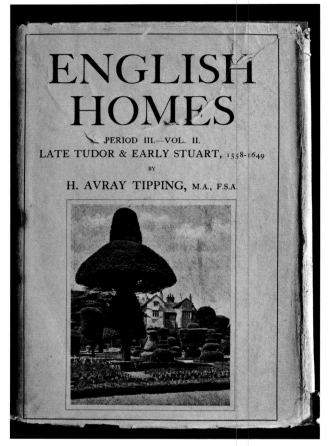

by train from Chepstow, visiting the Country Life offices in Tavistock Street, Covent Garden and working on articles in the British Museum and London Library. He stayed at the old Conservative Club in St James's, or sometimes with Edward Hudson at 15 Queen Anne's Gate, and lunched and dined with friends or colleagues, including Gertrude Jekyll, Edwin Lutyens, William Robinson, Lawrence Weaver and Celia Congreve. He also stayed with the owners of country houses about which he was writing articles: Henry Seymour Trower at Bridge House near Weybridge, the Maryon-Wilsons at Charlton House in Greenwich and Wickham Flower at Great Tangley Manor, Surrey. While in London he visited the Royal Horticultural Society shows at the Inner Temple Grounds, attended exhibitions, viewed furniture at the auction houses, and enjoyed theatre trips particularly plays by George Bernard Shaw.

Between 1904 and 1909 Tipping edited *In English Homes* in which Charles Latham's sumptuous photographs formed 'an unparalleled pictorial survey of the domestic architecture of England'. Tipping's passion for the architecture of Vanburgh shines through in his books and his own houses. However his book *The Work of Sir John Vanburgh and his School 1699–1736*, a collaboration with Christopher Hussey and the last in his mammoth series *English Homes*, did not appear until 1928.

In 1908 Tipping edited the third volume of *Gardens Old & New* for the Country Life Library, replacing John Leyland who had edited the first two. The *Daily Chronicle* wrote in review,

The accounts of lovely garden after lovely garden are most agreeable reading. There is no country in the world where managed sylvan beauty can be found

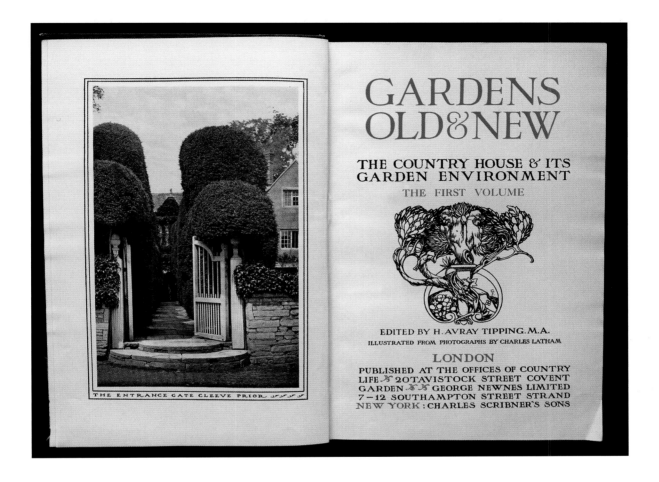

THE ENTRANCE GATE CLEEVE PRIOR

GARDENS
OLD & NEW

THE COUNTRY HOUSE & ITS
GARDEN ENVIRONMENT

THE FIRST VOLUME

EDITED BY H. AVRAY TIPPING. M.A.
ILLUSTRATED FROM PHOTOGRAPHS BY CHARLES LATHAM

LONDON
PUBLISHED AT THE OFFICES OF COUNTRY
LIFE 20 TAVISTOCK STREET COVENT
GARDEN GEORGE NEWNES LIMITED
7–12 SOUTHAMPTON STREET STRAND
NEW YORK : CHARLES SCRIBNER'S SONS

comparable to this in England, and as albums of charming pictures for the garden lovers and a mine of elegant suggestion to the garden-maker, these volumes are the best thing of their kind we have ever seen.

In 1909 he wrote *A Short History of Kensington Square* for Owen Grant, the antique dealer whose premises were at Nos 11 and 12, together with drawings by Kitchin and photographs of their current stock of furniture. Tipping wrote,

Nos. 11 and 12 are in the hands of Messrs. Owen Grant Ltd, not only is everyone of their original features sure of loving preservation, but the fine examples of furniture and decorative object – so many of them contemporary with the building – which they place in the rooms, complete the picture of the past and make it a place of pilgrimage for those who desire to live again for a moment in the days of the last of the Stuarts and the first of the Hanoverians.

Tipping and Kitchin may have bought furniture from Owen Grant for their own houses.

When his brother William Fearon died in 1911, leaving him real and personal estate to the value of £250,000, Tipping inherited the entire Brasted estate. The next year,

OPPOSITE LEFT Front cover of *In English Homes*, published in 3 volumes by Country Life Ltd.
OPPOSITE RIGHT One volume, with dust cover, of Tipping's magnum opus, the 9 volume series of *English Homes*.
ABOVE *Gardens Old & New*. Tipping was credited as editor for all three volumes in later editions.

having by then committed himself to Monmouthshire, he put the whole demesne up for sale. The mansion standing in 120 acres of parkland contained 22 bed and dressing rooms, stabling for 7 horses, motor home, model farm and beautiful old gardens. The complete estate extended to 650 acres, including a proposed 18 hole golf course, on which in 1911 Tipping had taken the advice of James Braid from Walton Heath Golf Club who reported, 'I have carefully gone over the land available for a golf course at Brasted Place, and find it is admirably adapted for the making of a good course'. The auction on 11 June 1912 included at least 50 village houses, the water mill and the White Hart Inn, but the mansion itself was not sold, and a sale total of just over £8,000 was realised. The house was eventually acquired by Leslie Urquhart,

Final Edition.

By direction of the Executor of the late Colonel W. FEARON TIPPING.

KENT

Between Sevenoaks and Westerham

The Beautiful Freehold
and Residential Estate

KNOWN AS

BRASTED PLACE

Situate in the pretty Kentish Village of Brasted, about one mile from the Station, four miles from Sevenoaks, two miles from Westerham, and extending to about

650 ACRES

Mostly in Brasted Parish, but partly in that of Sundridge, including

The MANSION, standing in a finely timbered Park of 120 Acres and containing six Reception Rooms, 22 Bed and Dressing Rooms, two Bathrooms, Stabling for seven horses, Motor House, etc., Model Home Farm, and Beautiful Old Gardens.

Also 18-HOLE GOLF COURSE has been planned under the advice of James Braid. Home Farm and densely timbered Woodlands. Several excellent Private Residences, Village Shops, Water Mill, and numerous Cottages, which

Messrs. KNIGHT, FRANK & RUTLEY

have been instructed to offer by Auction as a whole, or in Lots, on TUESDAY, 11th JUNE, 1912, at THE VILLAGE HALL, BRASTED, commencing at TWO o'clock precisely (unless previously sold by Private Treaty).

Solicitors:

Messrs. CORBOULD, RIGBY & Co.
1, HENRIETTA STREET
CAVENDISH SQUARE, LONDON, W.

Auctioneers & Land Agents:

Messrs. KNIGHT, FRANK & RUTLEY
20, HANOVER SQUARE, LONDON, W.,
Who will issue Orders to View.

a distinguished mine owner, engineer and sportsman. In recent years Brasted Place has been opened as a pre-theological college for students for the Anglican ministry but has now been converted into seven apartments.

Tipping's mother, Maria, also died at the end of 1911, the same year as the last of his brothers, and many items from the family collection of paintings, porcelain and silver that Tipping did not want to keep were put up for auction. He presented the British Museum with a Ming celadon dish. He gave his terracotta model of Chaloner Chute, the Speaker of the House of Commons in 1659, to the Victoria and Albert Museum in 1911, still housed in its original leather case. This monument, carved by Thomas Carter in 1775 for the chapel attached to the Vyne in Hampshire, is described by Rupert Gunnis in his *Dictionary of British Sculptors* as 'one of the noblest works of late eighteenth-century sculpture in England'. Tipping had written articles for *Country Life* about the Vyne and presumably acquired the full-scale model, showing the Speaker reclining on a woven pallet, his head resting on his right hand, with his hat and book by his side, around this time. The monument was placed in the chapel at the same time as Chute's friend Horace Walpole was setting the windows with medieval glass. Tipping also contributed money, along with the National Arts Collection Fund, Sir William Lever and Sir George Riddell, for the purchase of the Hatton Garden Room, a complete panelled chamber dating from the early years of George III's reign which was donated to the Victoria and Albert Museum. Thus Tipping's writings

OPPOSITE LEFT The sale particulars of the Tipping family home, Brasted Place in Kent, in 1912.
OPPOSITE RIGHT Thomas Carter's monument to Chaloner Chute, *1775*, in the chapel at the Vyne in Hampshire.
LEFT Tipping's London home, 11 Dorset Square, Marylebone, where he held dinner parties for G.H. Kitchin, Harold Peto, Percy Macquoid and the Editor of the *Morning Post*, H.A. Gwynne.
BELOW Mounton House, built in 1911–12, a collaboration with architect E.C. Francis.

LEFT Tipping's horse and carriage at Mathern Palace in 1908, driven by T. Cooke. BELOW Frontispiece from *The Story of the Royal Welsh Fusiliers* showing 'Private. Royal Welsh Fusiliers, 1742', painted by G.H. Kitchin. RIGHT Illustration of the west chimneypiece of the saloon at Belton House in Lincolnshire from Tipping's *Grinling Gibbons and the Woodwork of his Age.*

and beneficence played an important role in encouraging interest in an earlier English past.

In 1911 Tipping bought 11 Dorset Square as his London headquarters and in the same year he bought the land above the limestone gorge at Mounton where he had already created his water garden. Here, on the bare hilltop site, he started an ambitious building project and his most important home, Mounton House, where he was to live for ten years and to lay out splendid formal gardens. By this time he was travelling throughout England and Wales, at first by railway or horse and carriage, visiting country houses and gardens for his almost weekly articles. It is said that there was hardly an historic house throughout Britain that he did not visit at least once. After 1912 he bought his own motor car and employed a chauffeur to drive him on

these trips since he had lost an eye at some time during the First World War. It was in 1912 that he received his most important commission when Sir Arthur Lee asked him to design the gardens at Chequers in Buckinghamshire. This led to further commissions for Hubert Delaval Astley at Brinsop Court in Herefordshire, where he supervised the restoration of the house, and Charles Clay at Wyndcliffe Court near Chepstow, where he designed the garden. His advice was also sought by Ernest and Dorothy Elmhirst at Dartington Hall, and friends at Yews in Cumbria (Sir Samuel Scott), Gregynog (Margaret and Gwendoline Davies) and Buckland Hall (Mrs Gwynne-Holford) in Powys.

Tipping's first abiding interest was wood carving, particularly the work of Grinling Gibbons, and in 1914 he wrote the first study on Gibbons's work, *Grinling Gibbons and the Woodwork of his Age*. This book, with its detailed descriptions of his best work, was a comprehensive account of the golden age of wood carving in England. In 1915 Tipping wrote for the Country Life Military History series *The Story of the Royal Welsh Fusiliers*, perhaps as a patriotic wartime gesture but probably because his brother William Fearon had been involved with the regiment, also to highlight its long and honourable record and to include a Roll of Honour for the first year of the Great War. Charles Oman, the military historian, reviewed the book, writing,

> Mr. Tipping knows how to write a story and (what is not quite the same thing) how to write a book. Furthermore he approaches regimental history in the right spirit, as part of the history alike of the Army and the Empire. Altogether the book is well written, well arranged and well produced.

High Glanau Chepstow from the South. July 4. 26.

As well as writing on houses and gardens for *Country Life* Tipping was contributing articles on furniture to the *Burlington Magazine* and penning reviews of 'English Furniture at the Burlington Fine Art Club'. His book *English Furniture of the Cabriole Period* was published in 1922 and he gave charity lectures on the furniture of the Stuart period at Lansdowne House and at 38 South Street, the home of The Hon. Henry McLaren (later Lord Aberconway).

The following year (1923), Tipping gave away Mounton House to his brother's godson, Hubert Holden, who lived there until the late 1930s (William Fearon Tipping had specifically requested in his will that Hubert Holden should receive some property). Harry Tipping by then had bought 18,000 acres of the Trellech estate from the Duke of Beaufort and set about building a new house, High Glanau near Monmouth, and laying out its gardens. It would seem that once he had finished a house and garden, he was restless to start a new challenge and would move on to another project.

Although Tipping was known foremost as a historian, he was also a practical gardener and knowledgeable plantsman. In his book *The Garden of To-day*, published in 1933, he wrote,

I was given a garden when I was seven. I am now seventy-seven and I still garden. During three score and ten years I have made and maintained gardens. Experience, therefore, I have, and I trust some of it has been transformed into fruitful knowledge.

Besides studying and practising horticultural techniques, he had taken training in architecture. In pursuing these interests he found a kindred spirit in Harold Peto (1854–1933), an active architect and garden designer. Peto's father, like Tipping's, was a wealthy railway magnate. In 1876 Peto went into partnership with Ernest George (1839–1922) and the practice became one of the most fashionable in London, with Lutyens, Herbert Baker, Robert Weir Schultz and Guy Dawber becoming assistants there. Tipping and Peto chanced upon Iford Manor in Wiltshire together, about which discovery Tipping wrote,

> I well remember, when on a bicycle tour, happening upon the place standing half derelict, and being charmed, even in the condition in which I found it, by its splendid hanging woods, its stately terrace walk, its interesting house with so much history in a medley of styles.

By 1899 Peto had acquired the house and transformed its garden on an Italian theme, already made popular by Charles A. Platt's *Italian Gardens* published in 1894. Peto wrote in his journal *The Boke of Iford*,

Old buildings or fragments of masonry carry one's mind back to the past in a way that a garden of flowers only cannot do. Gardens that are too stony are equally unsatisfactory: it is the combination of the two in just proportion which is the most satisfactory.

At Iford there is a series of delectable terraces, an oval pool and octagonal summerhouse, broad walks set high on the steep hillside, a loggia with pillars of Verona marble, a well

LEFT Pencil sketch of High Glanau in 1926 by G.H. Kitchin.
BELOW Harold Ainsworth Peto photographed in 1907 at home at Iford Manor, Wiltshire.

head and curved stone seat informally planted with wisteria, cypress and yew. It was the ideal location for Peto to introduce the architectural fragments and sculptures acquired on his travels. The garden is a tribute to his Arts and Crafts approach to design and Tipping wrote with great admiration about it in *Country Life* in 1910, 'if the relative spheres and successful inter-marriage of formal and natural gardening are better understood today than ever before, that desirable result is due to the efforts of no one man more than to Mr. Peto'.

Tipping often stayed at Iford, signing the visitors book four times in both 1899 and 1900, significantly the most important years of the garden's creation, and most years thereafter up to 1924. Peto in turn frequently stayed with Tipping in Monmouthshire. Ralph Edwards the furniture expert at the Victoria and Albert Museum remembered Peto as,

The British aesthete – in pose, appearance and voice. Verging on old age when I met him, he had been

granted plenty of time to study the part. I recall him at dinner in Dorset Square [Tipping's house] with his fastidious air and mincing gait, cambric ruffles at his wrists, his manner and deportment evoking contemporary descriptions of Horace Walpole.

Peto, like Tipping, also collected old furniture, some of which was bequeathed to the Victoria and Albert Museum. Peto had been best man to Percy Macquoid, who after 1911 joined Tipping at *Country Life* to contribute articles on furniture, and he would have been a frequent visitor with Tipping to Macquoid's home in Bayswater to admire his furniture collection. Peto's most important garden commissions are Wayford Manor in Somerset, Easton Lodge in Essex, Heale House in Wiltshire, Buscot Park in Berkshire and Garinish Island in County Cork. In 1892 Peto severed his partnership with Ernest George, which meant he could not practise as an architect in Britain, so he worked on the Côte d'Azur, designing some of the most enchanting villa gardens for wealthy expatriates. In 1902 he designed the Villa Sylvia as a winter home for the painter Ralph Curtis, whom he had met on a visit

LEFT Iford Manor and bridge over the river Frome.
ABOVE The cloister at Iford completed in 1914.
RIGHT View through the colonnade from the Casita at Iford.

to Boston with Henry James. Then in 1904 he created the Villa Rosemary for Mrs Arthur Cohen and in 1910 the Villa Maryland for Mr and Mrs Arthur Wilson, as well as laying out their gardens. These hillside gardens are dotted with olive trees, cypress, marble lined pools, and pergolas with vistas to the turquoise sea below. Peto was probably at his creative best on the French Riviera. He was creating gardens when the area was at its height of fashion and Bernard Berenson, the American art historian, staying at Villa Sylvia in 1911, greatly admired his creation calling it,

A dream of loveliness. Between Ralph's taste and attention and the incredible willingness of the soil and climate, floral miracles are performed here daily.

Tipping gave a glimpse of the charmed life of leisure enjoyed by the wealthy visitors to warmer climes when he wrote in *Country Life* in 1912,

There will be a great foregathering of English folk on the Riviera this Eastertide for it is then that the statue of Queen Victoria is to be unveiled and that of King Edward at Cannes. Then, too, the harbour of Villefranche is to be the scene of a meeting of the fleets of the *entente cordiale* group, France acting as hostess to her Russian and English friends.

Peto was working in the South of France at the same time as Cecil Pinsent (1884–1963) was designing gardens for the English and American émigrés in their villas around

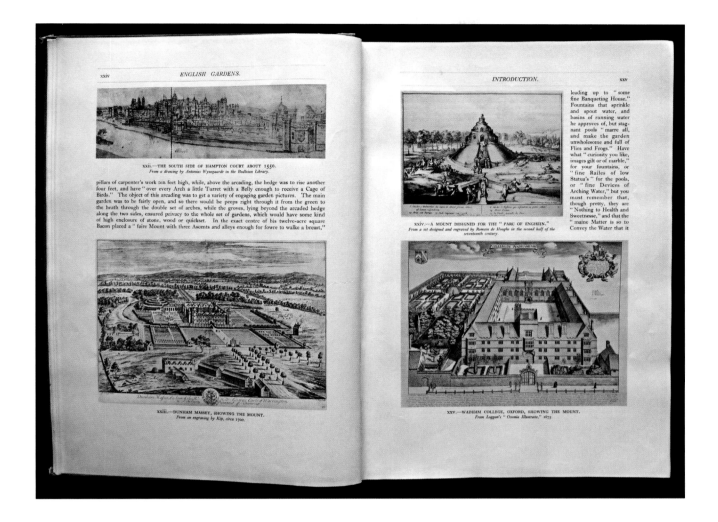

LEFT The square columned pergola at Villa Rosemary, Cap Ferrat, built by Peto in 1904 for Mr and Mrs Arthur Cohen.

ABOVE Pages from the introduction of Tipping's book on garden history, *English Gardens*, 1925.

Florence. His partner was Geoffrey Scott (1883–1929) who wrote *The Architecture of Humanism*, a book that Tipping was often to quote. It is tempting to speculate that Peto and Tipping may have known these younger men working in the same field.

In 1925 Tipping published *English Gardens*, the first Country Life folio to present the history of gardens, starting from Westbury Court and Canons Ashby right through to Munstead Wood, Iford Manor and Lutyens's Hestercombe. In this book he really enjoyed championing the gardens of his friends: William Robinson's Gravetye, G.H. Kitchin's Compton End, Miss Willmott's Warley Place, as well as his own at Mathern Palace and Mounton. These were all written up with fine photographs. Also in 1925 he lectured on Gertrude Jekyll, now in her

eighty-fourth year, to the newly founded Garden Club with its headquarters in Mayfair.

In 1927 the National Gardens Scheme was set up, originally called 'The Gardens of England and Wales Scheme'. Tipping was a member of the first committee, headed by Hilda, Duchess of Richmond and Gordon, with Miss Wagg, Lady Georgina Mure, Mrs Frank Stobart, Mrs Pepyat Evans and Sir William Lawrence, treasurer and council member of the Royal Horticultural Society. King

The

Royal Horticultural Society's

INTERNATIONAL EXHIBITION OF GARDEN DESIGN & CONFERENCE

IN THE SOCIETY'S HALLS,

Vincent Square and Greycoat Street,
Westminster, S.W. 1,

FROM OCTOBER 17th TO OCTOBER 24th,
1928.

—

ADMISSION.

Season Tickets	- - - - -	10/6

Fellows' Tickets admit Free.

Wednesday,	October 17th.	10 a.m. to 6 p.m. -	7/6
Thursday,	October 18th.	10 a.m. to 6 p.m. -	5/–
Friday,	October 19th.	10 a.m. to 6 p.m. -	5/–
Saturday,	October 20th.	10 a.m. to 6 p.m. -	2/6
Monday,	October 22nd.	10 a.m. to 6 p.m. -	1/6
Tuesday,	October 23rd.	10 a.m. to 6 p.m. -	1/6
Wednesday,	October 24th.	10 a.m. to 5 p.m. -	1/6

CONFERENCE.

Lectures on October 18th, 19th, 22nd and 23rd.

See page 11.

11

Conference.

The Conference will be held in the Lecture Room
of the New Hall, Greycoat Street,
Westminster, S.W.1.

WEDNESDAY, OCTOBER 17th.
Opening Ceremony by the Rt. Hon. the   11.30 a.m.
EARL OF CRAWFORD & BALCARRES, K.T., F.R.S.

THURSDAY, OCTOBER 18th.
Mr. Avray Tipping : 'The Garden of Pleasure in England
from Plantagenet to Victorian Times' ...   ...12 noon.
Chairman : The Rt. Hon. Viscount Ullswater, G.C.B.
Monsieur Duchene : 'French Gardens' ...   . 3 p.m.
Chairman : His Grace the Duke of Marlborough,
K.G., P.C., T.D.
Miss Gertrude Jekyll : 'Colour in Garden Planning' and
Mr. Gilbert Jenkins, F.R.I.B.A.: 'Recent Developments in
Garden Design' ...   . 4 p.m.
Chairman : Sir Lawrence Weaver, K.B.E.

FRIDAY, OCTOBER 19th.
Mr. Gilbert Bayes : 'Fountains and Garden Sculpture'...12 noon.
Chairman : Major-General Lord Edward Gleichen,
K.C.V.O., C.B., C.M.G., D.S.O.
Dr. C. Schneider : 'A Modern Park, more particularly the
Park of Graf E. Silva Tarouca at Pruhonice, near
Prague'...   ...   . 3 p.m.
Chairman : Mr. Mark Fenwick.
Mr. Leonard Barron : 'American Gardens' ...   ... 4 p.m.
Chairman : Lady Isabel Margesson.

MONDAY, OCTOBER 22nd.
Mr. G. Dillistone : 'Small English Gardens' ...   ... 12 noon.
Chairman : Sir Oscar E. Warburg, O.B.E.
Mr. J. R. Koning : 'Dutch Gardens' ...   . 3 p.m.
Chairman : Sir William Lawrence, Bt.
Mr. C. Hussey : 'Garden Ornaments' ...   . 4 p.m.
Chairman : Lord Stanmore, C.V.O.

TUESDAY, OCTOBER 23rd.
Mr. E. P. Mawson : 'Modern Tendencies in the Design and
Equipment of Public Parks' ...   . 12 noon.
Chairman : Sir Lionel Earle, K.C.B., K.C.V.O.,
C.M.G., J.P.
Mr. W. W. Pettigrew : 'Lantern Exhibition of Public
Parks and Gardens' ...   . 3 p.m.
Chairman : Mr. E. White, V.M.H.

ABOVE LEFT The International Exhibition of Garden Design in 1928.
ABOVE RIGHT List of distinguished lecturers at the accompanying conference.
LEFT Photograph of the exhibition rooms showing the sculptures.

George V allowed his private garden at Sandringham to be opened. In addition those at Blenheim, Chatsworth, Hatfield and elsewhere those belonging to renowned gardeners, such as Robinson's Gravetye Manor and Miss Willmott's Warley Place, were opened to visitors at one shilling a head. In September 1929 Tipping opened his own garden at High Glanau for the same scheme and it is a tribute to his original design that it is still opened one day a year some eight decades later.

In June 1928 Tipping gave two lectures, illustrated by lantern slides lent by *Country Life*, on, 'the nature and characteristics of the English Furniture of the past and on the value to our present needs and purposes of a serious study of it'. These were to coincide with the opening of Messrs Waring and Gillow's exhibition of, 'nineteen rooms illustrative of various styles of English decoration and furniture, the latter being composed of original pieces or of acknowledged reproductions'. His long lectures, which give a summary of the story of English furniture down to the classic activities of Robert Adam, show his profound range of knowledge, but he was still able to gauge the importance of aptly equipping a modern house to suit the domestic wants and purse of twentieth-century man. What was novel was the stimulating advice to the present generation which Tipping tells us has bestowed, 'unthinking worship upon ancient gear'. At the end of the lectures Tipping puts four important points to the audience:

> First of all, I would ask you to preserve, appreciate and study the old. Secondly, to avoid promiscuous purchase of what falsely passes for old, otherwise you will be supporting the manufacture of fakes, which are an unmitigated evil. Thirdly, to accept honest and acknowledged reproductions if you are set on exact models and cannot have really truthful old pieces. Fourthly, remember that your furniture should represent your present-day needs and tastes and cannot be quite wholesome and ring true unless it is designed on purpose, although on the basis of tradition.

These lectures attracted a large audience and so much appreciation that Country Life printed them as a book *Old English Furniture – Its true value and function*. So once again we see Tipping educating the audience and setting standards of taste.

In 1928 the Council of the Royal Horticultural Society organised an International Exhibition of Garden Design and a Conference on garden planning. Tipping was on the committee as chairman of the 'Retrospective Historical Section up to 1850' with Edward Hudson and Christopher Hussey. He was invited to give the first of a series of lectures during the exhibition. Other lecturers were Monsieur Duchêne, who had recently designed the water terraces at Blenheim, on 'French Gardens', Gertrude Jekyll on 'Colour in Garden Planning', Christopher Hussey on 'Garden Ornaments' and Edward Mawson on public parks. Tipping was introduced by the chairman, the Rt Hon. Viscount Ullswater, GCB, as 'the greatest authority in England upon the subject on which he will address you'. Tipping spoke on 'The Garden of Pleasure in England from Plantagenet to Victorian Times'. He urged the audience to look at, 'the large collection of representations of English gardens hung on the walls to indicate the various phases through which garden craft has passed in this country' and he used lantern slides, again lent by *Country Life*, to illustrate the alluring gardens of Althorp, Petworth, Denham Place, Holme Lacey and Chatsworth. The exhibition included illuminated manuscripts, John Smithson's plans of Wollaton and Ham, drawings, Kip's bird's-eye views of Hampton Court in Herefordshire and Longleat, pictures of Claremont by Roque kindly lent by Lady Chichester, statues by Van Nost, sculptured vases, books, including *Britannia Illustrata*, and John Tradescant's accounts showing how he travelled and what he bought in France, Flanders and Holland as stock for the Lord Treasurer Salisbury's garden. The main hall of the exhibition even included modern stone sculptures such as *Silence* by William Reid Dick (1879–1961) and a bronze *Hope* by W. Reynolds-Stephens (1862–1943). Tipping concluded his lecture by appealing to his audience,

> What I ask you to do, in gardening as in other arts and crafts, is to get a thorough knowledge of the rich past into which I have sought to give you a peep. But look round at the present and create a garden that retains some flavour

of antiquity and yet uses intelligently and tastefully all that to-day gives you of new forms and new groupings, of choice introduction and beautiful hybrids.

Sir William Lawrence, in thanking him, felt that the audience owed, 'a real depth of gratitude to Mr. Avray Tipping for giving them something to think about, and when they go to see these houses (easily reached by car or char-a-banc) – nearly all of them are open on certain days of the week through the kindness of their owners – they will say "I remember what we heard at the lecture at the Royal Horticultural Society".'

In 1929 Tipping wrote *Tattershall Castle, Lincolnshire*. This book had been planned by Lord Curzon of Kedleston as a series of volumes on the ancient houses he owned. He had completed the one on Bodiam Castle, but for the Tattershall volume he had written no more than a pencilled draft of an introduction. Unfortunately his death cut short its completion. He had however collected considerable material which was entrusted to Tipping's care 'with the object of amplifying it and shaping it into a book'. Curzon had restored the castle with the help of William Weir, and bequeathed it to the National Trust on his death in 1925. William Weir (1865–1950) was deeply involved with the Society for the Preservation of Ancient Buildings, and concerned with more than three hundred projects of repair of ancient structures. He had worked with Tipping on the restoration of Brinsop Court and Dartington Hall. Tipping concluded the two hundred pages of the book from Curzon's notes with photographs and Weir's plans, and, in addition, the Cromwell papers documenting the building of the castle by Cromwell which Tipping found only after Curzon's death.

On 25 March 1930 Tipping again addressed the Royal Horticultural Society; by this time he was seventy-five. Mark Fenwick was chairman, and Tipping lectured specifically on 'English Garden Making under the Early Stuarts'. He described the profusion of great gardens of this period and explained that the early half of the seventeenth century was a peaceful time in England, the leading personages were wealthy and Audley End and Hatfield were built. Knole and Bramshill were developed. There was also garden literature by this date; Thomas Hill had extended the *Brief and Pleasaunt Treatyse* which he printed in 1563 into the *Gardener's Labyrinth* and John Gerarde brought out his *Herbal* in 1597. An English edition of Crispin de Passe's *Hortus Floridus* appeared in 1616, by which time Bacon was considering his *Essay on Gardens*. William Lawson had his *New Orchard* ready for the printer, and John Parkinson was growing the plants and making the notes that formed his *Paradisus* published in 1612.

Robert Cecil had by then, he continued, become Lord Treasurer to James I and joined a deep knowledge of home affairs with a wide continental outlook, so in buildings and garden making, as well as politics and diplomacy, he created the fashion for new developments. Suddenly galleries, open or closed, bounded the garden on one or more sides; terraces lay in front of the house or might

LEFT William Weir in his mid-twenties with his penny-farthing. As a conservation architect, he upheld the principles of the SPAB with almost fanatical sincerity.
RIGHT Tipping (second right) aged seventy-five with Mrs Gwynne-Holford and family at Hartpury, Gloucestershire, in 1930. Tipping advised Mrs Gwynne-Holford on this garden and at Buckland Hall in Powys.

surround sunken portions of the garden; great fountains occupied important points and there would be squares of topiary work and knots of flowers and herbs. Tipping used Bolsover, Thorpe Hall, Ham and Hatfield as examples, having already written up these great houses for *Country Life* and in 1927 Country Life Ltd had published his Late Tudor and Early Stuart volume of *English Homes*.

While keeping his country house in Monmouthshire, Tipping moved from his hospitable house in Dorset Square in London, to what Christopher Hussey called, 'an unprepossessing house and property' at Harefield in Middlesex. Nikolaus Pevsner only gives it a cursory glance in his book on Middlesex, but does offer a clue as to what may have brought Tipping to Harefield. The parish church contained more funeral monuments that any church of similar size anywhere near London; 'the chancel especially is as cram-full of curious objects as the rooms of the Soane Museum', noted Pevsner, including some

carved by Grinling Gibbons, Tipping's enduring interest. With the help of ten gardeners, Tipping transformed the grounds of his new home with many exotic shrubs and flowers. Hussey records,

> Within a few years the place was unrecognisable. What had been dishevelled meadows had become spacious gardens, where broad grass vistas were flanked by formal *bosquets* of flowering shrubs planted in bold masses. The Harefield garden was, perhaps, his greatest *tour de force* and, incidentally, proved the soundness of his dictum that trenching to a depth of three spits will double the annual growth of shrubs. The beds at Harefield were, outwardly, a litter of stones and gravel. But everything grew with tropical rapidity.

The plant collector E.H.M. Cox remembers 'four square beds of the old-fashioned fringed pinks, scenting the

heavens, set in plain regular paving against a background of ordinary blue lupins, a combination as completely satisfying to all the senses as I have ever met with'. Ralph Edwards, who thought the house, 'rather common-place', records that Tipping, 'laid out another delightful garden, conjuring it into existence with phenomenal speed and triumphing over the daunting character of the flat and featureless grounds'.

In 1933 he designed four estate houses on the northern boundary of Harefield House. Two were large, Little Hammonds and Walnut Trees (this one demolished in 1960), and two smaller servantless houses. These were illustrated in *Country Life* in April 1934 in an article by Randall Philips, who wrote, 'Mr. Tipping was not only a distinguished authority on the design and history of the great houses of England, their gardens and their furniture, but was also fully informed about what may be called the average house of to-day'. These houses were designed by Tipping without an architect, and they combine efficiency

TOP Pencil sketch of Harefield House, Middlesex, in 1927 by G.H. Kitchin.

ABOVE Presentation of the Tipping Trophy at the Harefield School Sports Day held in the gardens at Harefield House in 1934.

and convenience as well as economy. The larger ones built of brick with steel casements were, 'not over-costly to build, economical to maintain, and convenient for everyday running'. The smaller houses, each of which was completed for less than £750 including garden making, roadway and fencing, were noteworthy in having three bedrooms and a large sitting room extending the whole width of the garden front. These were illustrated in 1936 in *Houses for Moderate Means* published by Country Life.

In the last years of his life there were only a few articles in *Country Life*, possibly because visits to London and the libraries were more difficult. His friends were dying – Percy Macquoid in 1925, Lawrence Weaver in 1930, Gertrude Jekyll in 1932 and Harold Peto in 1933. He was content to be at home, mostly at Harefield with spring and summer visits to High Glanau, and concentrating on his gardens and writing about gardening. During his lifetime Tipping's literary output was prolific. Over and above his twenty-one books and hundreds of *Country Life* articles, from 1928 until 1933 he contributed a weekly column on practical gardening published each Sunday in the *Observer*. It was these articles

that brought his name to a much wider public. He offered practical tips about tried and tested plants according to the season: hydrangeas from China, North America and Japan, wild gardening and water-loving plants, perennials, annuals, shrubs, fruit and herbs. He recommended nurseries, the fortnightly shows at the Royal Horticultural Society, places to visit and he gave expert advice on nurturing plants, often citing his gardens in Monmouthshire or Middlesex. In the winter he occasionally wrote the column on garden history subjects. He always wrote with a distinct love of flowers, noted in 1933 by Lady Congreve in her recollection,

> He did not love flowers only in bulk, he loved each one individually – he always held a flower as if he loved it. A weed was not a crime, and in autumn he liked the leaves to lie about until they were all down; but in planning great masses and stretches of colour for all seasons of the year he had no rival.

He often gathered flowers himself, for vases in the house to appreciate their full beauty near at hand.

From 1930 he also wrote a Saturday page for the *Morning Post*. This included an article on the culture of plants and to illustrate the point he was making he added photographs of his own ornamental grounds or those of his friends: Sir Martin Conway's Allington Castle, Lawrence Johnston's

BELOW Little Hammonds in Harefield (left) designed by Tipping in 1933 and Pear Trees (right), one of a pair of small servantless houses designed by Tipping in 1933 for less than £750.

Hidcote, Detmar Blow's Wilsford Manor, Clough Williams-Ellis's Oare House, Harold Peto's Garinish Island, Nathaniel Lloyd's Great Dixter, often Lutyens and Jekyll gardens and several times Ellen Willmott's own photographs of Warley Place. He answered readers' queries and identified plants they sent him,

C.H.H. – Greengages are shy bearers unless the soil is a deep, rather stiff, but well-drained soil with some lime. The Victoria plum is a great cropper as a rule. It may be better for root pruning next winter. Avoid horse manure unless very well rotted. Cox's Pippin is another shy bearer unless the soil exactly suits it. For the rhododendrons see cultural remarks in the issue of May 24. AVOID horse manure.

Garden Lover – The flower is that of a parrot tulip, of which various varieties are given in all bulb catalogues. Cut away the old and shabby shoots of Butcher's Broom (*Ruscus aculeatus*) now that this year's have come up.

He then added a section on 'Next Week in the Garden', listing jobs to be done and warning of greenfly on rose bushes and giving remedies for mildew, with instructions to spray with slum and lead arsenate powder. This page had advertisements for Barr's Seeds, Kelway's glorious Gladioli, Green's mowers that gave that 'velvet' touch to the lawn, Windolite cloches and Original Wakeley's Hop Manure.

In the last year of his life, aged seventy-eight, Tipping wrote *The Garden of To-day* which was a practical

gardening book containing material used in his *Morning Post* columns, but refashioned and rewritten. This book was published by Martin Hopkinson Ltd not Country Life Ltd, perhaps because he did not want to tread on Gertrude Jekyll's toes.

In 1930 Tipping had undertaken his last venture: to make a landscape water garden in a fold of the bleak Cotswold plateau at Old Chalford near Chipping Norton. This had originally been part of the Heythrop estate

which featured a classical grove with rill, cold bath and cascade much admired by Switzer and noted in 1718 in his *Ichnographia Rustica*. Heythrop belonged to Albert Brassey, son of another railway pioneer and friend of Tipping, and Brassey must have sold Tipping the land through which the river Glyme ran, together with an old farmhouse. The river which flowed through both Blenheim and Heythrop must have presented Tipping with a last thrilling challenge to create a fascinating water garden. Christopher Hussey remembered visiting,

LEFT The Saturday gardening page of the *Morning Post*.
BELOW The design for the garden at Compton End by G.H. Kitchin which Tipping used for the endpapers of his last book, *The Garden of To-day*.

Alas! He was overtaken by his last illness before the project had more than half matured, though, when he took one round the yet virgin meadows and explained his intentions with his customary vividness and

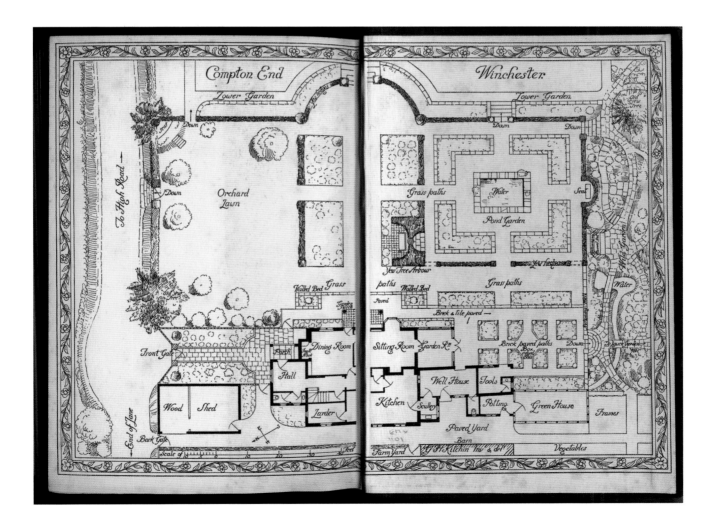

enthusiasm, it was almost possible to see what, in fact, will never be realised.

In November 1933 Tipping died from cancer at Harefield House in Middlesex. In his obituary in the *Uxbridge Advertiser and Gazette* a local resident wrote,

By the passing of Mr. H. Avray Tipping, Harefield loses its greatest benefactor of recent times. Coming to Harefield some eleven years ago he took up residence at Harefield House. He enlarged the grounds and with that skill in all matters concerning gardens for which he was so justly famous, transformed them as by a fairy wand into a garden of exquisite taste and beauty. With a generosity too rarely met with in these days, he placed these delightful grounds at the disposal of the village for fetes, sports and the annual flower show. There is not an organisation in the village, but will feel keenly the loss. The Allotment Club was an association in which he took a keen personal interest, providing special accommodation for the storing of their supply of seed potatoes and giving the use of his grounds for their annual show. The British Legion received many marks of his favour, for he provided and maintained excellent cricket and football grounds, and gave generously to their building fund. The village Nursing Fund, the Choral Society and the church too held their fetes and sales of work in the gardens. The schoolchildren were ever welcome visitors on the occasions of their displays of drill and dancing, and nothing seemed to give him greater pleasure than watching these happy youngsters in such a delightful setting as was afforded by his beautiful grounds. In many ways Mr. Tipping was almost a recluse, and one who loved to do good by stealth, desiring no thanks, beyond seeing, as he once put it – 'the villagers doing things themselves for their own pleasure and amusement, and not looking for others to provide them.'

Christopher Hussey wrote of his fortitude in *Country Life*,

He reminded one of a fallen tree, during his last illness which, though fully aware of its incurable nature,

he refused to give in to and bore with much of his old breezy humour. To talk with him then, still fully dressed and vigorous of mind, though painfully weak, was indeed to be reminded of some hedge-row giant laid low, seen to be all the greater for its proneness. Whether as gardener, *savant*, or friend, it was above all his generous zest that infected all who had to do with him and will long keep his memory green, deep-trenched in their hearts.

Tipping's funeral was on 20 November in Harefield Church; the service, which was a simple one, at his express wish, was attended by a large and distinguished congregation. Mr Gwynne (editor of the *Morning Post*), Mr Humphrey Scott (representing the Society for the Preservation of Ancient Buildings), Mr Calkin (the manager of *Country Life*), Ralph Edwards (the Victoria and Albert Museum), Eric Francis (architect of Mounton and High Glanau), Col. Battye (furniture collector) and Aylmer Clerk (his solicitor) were all present. His friends Christopher Hussey (his successor at *Country Life*) with his widowed mother Mrs Mary Hussey, George Herbert Kitchin, Mrs Eardley-Wilmot and Mrs Stansfeld (relations of Sir Sam Scott, the owner of Yews in Cumbria), Lady Florence Pery, Major Hubert Holden (to whom Tipping gave Mounton House), Mrs Acland-Hood (whose garden Tipping designed) were there too. Also present were the architect Walter Sarel, Sir Francis and Lady Newdigate, his neighbours, and his staff from Harefield House, High Glanau and Old Chalford. There was also a long list of floral tributes including ones from Edward Hudson and his friends at Country Life Ltd and his many old friends in Monmouthshire, Kent and London.

Tipping left the residue of his estate and property, almost £100,000, to his head gardener, Walter Ernest Wood, aged thirty-one and the sum of £10,000 to Walter's brother William Henry Wood, chauffeur and valet, aged twenty-eight who had nursed him during his final illness. Speaking of this fortune to a *Daily Mail* reporter Walter Wood said,

Mr. Tipping treated my brother and myself almost as sons. He employed me shortly after the war as a gardener and I gradually worked my way up until I

ABOVE Pencil sketch of Harefield Church by G.H. Kitchin, 1928.
LEFT Interior of Harefield Church, to the right of the altar is the imposing tomb of Alice, Countess of Derby.

took charge of the nurseryman's business during Mr. Tipping's illness. My brother nursed him during the illness. We have made no plans yet. It is probable that the two estates [in Monmouthshire and Oxfordshire] will be sold.

Two other employees, Thomas Nelmes of Harefield and Albert Crocket his estate man at Mounton, received legacies of £1,000. Ralph Edwards in an article in *Apollo* remembers Walter Wood at Harefield House,

In the evenings, after coffee, drinks were dispensed to whoever might be staying in the house, the gardener responsible for much that made the

ABOVE A rare photograph of Walter Ernest Wood, Tipping's gardener at Harefield to whom he left a fortune.
RIGHT The Tipping family memorial at St Martin's Church, Brasted.
OPPOSITE Drawing of an enthusiastic architect and gardener by Hubert Astley, Tipping's former fellow thespian at OUDS and owner of Brinsop Court.

place attractive would suddenly appear in a lounge suit and be introduced to the company assembled in the hall; after this ceremony he would relapse in silence with his drink in the corner. One felt it was hospitality which he would have been glad to do without.

Walter Wood and Aylmer Clerk were executors and High Glanau and Old Chalford were sold, as well as much of Tipping's collection of furniture, paintings, silver and books. His painting *A Midsummer Afternoon with a Methodist Preacher*, a masterpiece by de Loutherbourg which hung above the fireplace at Harefield, now hangs in the National Gallery of Canada in Ottawa. Walter Wood was the last owner of the Harefield House estate and his benefactions to the village included a portion of the grounds for a cricket pitch. The house was put on the market in 1936, advertised as 'a charming old fashioned Gentleman's Residence'. The property included a picturesque lodge and excellent stabling, and a feature was made of the lawns and gardens with their fine cedar and elm trees and the brick-walled kitchen garden. Thus the last Tipping estate, with 21 acres, was on the market for an inclusive price of £9,000. In 1937 the property was purchased by His Majesty's Government for use by the Air Ministry as a Test House of the Aeronautical Inspection Directorate with ten acres of land for £4,750. Large laboratory buildings were built over Tipping's cherished gardens. Walter Wood moved to Hampshire and bought a farm, and burnt all Tipping's personal papers. The only known time he came back to Harefield was in 1967 for the opening of a new cricket pavilion on the Harefield ground.

Tipping was buried at St Martin's Church, Brasted, in the Stocket Chapel. His name was added to the Tipping memorial with his father and mother and his three brothers. He was the last of the Tipping dynasty.

"Here, to the left of the approach to the William Three façade, we could have a most amusing garden, don't you see?!!"

H Avray Tipping Esq,
Architect &
Landscape
Gardener

H.D.A
1915

An enthusiastic architect & gardener.

Tipping and colleagues at Country Life

I N THE LATE 1890S Tipping started writing articles for *The Garden*, a magazine founded by William Robinson in 1871 and to which Gertrude Jekyll had been a contributor since 1880. It is difficult to know exactly which articles he wrote as they were not attributed but his article on his own home, Mathern Palace, appeared in 1900, the year in which Jekyll was the editor with E.T. Cook. She must have introduced Tipping to Edward Hudson, the proprietor of *Country Life* as, soon after this, he joined the staff as staff architectural writer. From 1903 Tipping became a principal contributor to *Country Life*, transforming it from a country sportsman's journal in such a way that the country house and garden articles became its most characteristic feature.

Tipping's articles describing the social, historical and architectural development of each property in great detail were based on personal visits to each house and extensive research in public records, private collections and printed authorities. They were accompanied by lavish black and white photographs taken by Charles Latham or A.E. Henson. He signed most of his articles from 1907 onwards and assembled them into the nine impressive volumes of *English Homes*, which were published between 1920 and 1928. These became a standard reference for those studying the history of architecture and interior design and they constitute a lasting memorial. Seven hundred articles on country houses were written in the first nineteen years, with five hundred more by 1935. His successor Christopher Hussey acknowledges, 'Tipping brought to the writing of the articles an historical knowledge and an insistence on accuracy that gave them a new authoritativeness'. Hussey also records Tipping's interest in 'building craftsmanship', such that, 'his enthusiastic researches changed what had been a largely sentimental quest of the romantic and picturesque into a scientific study of the domestic arts as represented in the historic houses and gardens of England'.

Edward Hudson, the founder of *Country Life*, was born in November 1854 and took over his family printing company Hudson & Kearns at the age of twenty-one. He came

RIGHT Watercolour by Cyril Farey, FRIBA, of the new Country Life building in Tavistock Street designed by Lutyens in 1904.

into contact with Sir George Newnes (1851–1910), the son of a Congregationalist minister who had risen through the ranks of popular journalism. Newnes set up *Tit Bits* and they collaborated in the publication of *Navy and Army Illustrated*. Hudson and Newnes then acquired *Racing Illustrated*, which was then extended in 1897 to become *Country Life Illustrated*. Later the name was changed to *Country Life* and a public company Country Life Limited was formed in 1905. The original idea for the magazine was conceived on Walton Heath golf course with Hudson, Newnes and George Riddell (1865–1934), the son of a Brixton photographer who had climbed his way up in the legal profession to make his fortune with the *News of the World*. The first number was published on 8 January 1897. A notice announcing the launch of the magazine stated that, 'the finest pictorial printing machinery obtainable which has been specially built in America for the production of the paper, has been imported'.

Hudson insisted on high quality printing from half-tone blocks and, from the start, the magazine's impact was visual, rather than literary. Hudson was a perfectionist; his use of full-plate photographs to illustrate country houses and gardens made it the outstanding journal of the age. Bernard Darwin, the golf correspondent who wrote the first history of the magazine on the occasion of its fiftieth birthday wrote, 'The paper was the love of his life. Mr. Hudson was always the controller of the paper's policy from the earliest days and as long as he lived.' Although largely uneducated, as a young

OPPOSITE Studio portrait of Edward Hudson, founding publisher of *Country Life* magazine.
ABOVE LEFT William Robinson at the age of 84 in 1922.
ABOVE RIGHT Gertrude Jekyll as painted by Sir William Nicholson in 1920.

man Hudson was a great walker and keen golfer and he formed an obsession for country houses. Contact with William Robinson (Edward Hudson bought *The Garden* from him in 1900 and its offices were next door to *Country Life* at 10–11 Southampton Street off the Strand) and then Gertrude Jekyll initiated Hudson into the new gardening movement. His private life revolved largely around his friendship with Edwin Lutyens, whom he met at Miss Jekyll's house, and in 1899 he commissioned him to build the Deanery Garden, Sonning. This was one of the architect's first important buildings and combined

LEFT Portrait of Sir Edwin Lutyens as Master of the Art Workers Guild, 1933, by Meredith Frampton.

RIGHT The hall at Deanery Garden, built for Edward Hudson by Lutyens in 1901.

BELOW Looking towards Deanery Garden from the pergola above the circular pool. The garden was designed by Jekyll.

ABOVE Hudson's London home, 15 Queen Anne's Gate, with statue of Queen Anne outside
and Lutyens's house at number 17 on the right.
RIGHT Madame Suggia, the famous female cellist, painted by Augustus John, 1920–3.

traditional geometric design with Jekyll's naturalistic planting in a perfect balanced union. Hudson's London home was 15 Queen Anne's Gate, which he filled with exquisite furniture and paintings and where every room was like a picture. It continued to be his home after his marriage, late in life, to Miss Ellen Woolrich in 1929. This was the setting for lunch every Monday for *Country Life* contributors, always Lutyens, but often Tipping and Margaret Jourdain, the furniture expert who wrote 'Pages for the Connoisseur' for *Country Life*. Lutyens moved his office to 17 Queen Anne's Gate in 1910 and lunches and

dinners with his now neighbour Hudson soon became the rule. He was held in high esteem by Hudson and heavily promoted in the pages of *Country Life*, designing the magazine's new office in Covent Garden in 1904. He also restored Lindisfarne Castle in Northumberland for Hudson, making it one of the most romantic dwelling places in the country with Jekyll designing the garden there in 1911. Pamela Maude, who wrote 'Portrait of a perfectionist: Edward Hudson, the founder of *Country Life*', noted, 'Many of Hudson's happiest recollections centred round "the island" – the sea fishing expeditions,

BELOW Hudson's dream castle – Lindisfarne in Northumberland.

RIGHT Pencil sketch by G.H. Kitchin of Tipping sitting at a desk at Lindisfarne (also known as Holy Island) in 1907.

the hunts among the rocks for lobsters, the delightfully informal parties of clever and amusing people assembled in this unexpected setting'. Visitors, such as Madame Suggia, the great cellist and pupil and lover of Pablo Casals with whom Hudson shared his love of music, would give a full dress performance after dinner. Hudson commissioned a dashing portrait of her from Augustus John and may even have been engaged to her in 1919 when he gave her a 1717 Stradivarius cello. The marriage certainly never took place, perhaps because Hudson was significantly older, and probably she was convinced that her career ambitions were incompatible with marriage. He bequeathed £250 in his will to Suggia in appreciation of her 'valued friendship and glorious music'.

The Congreve and Lutyens families as well as Tipping and Kitchin all stayed with Hudson at Lindisfarne and when the tide covered the causeway they had to cross by boat. Lutyens, who was summoned to Lindisfarne by a 'dreadfully nervous Hudson' to get ready for a visit of the Prince and Princess of Wales in 1908, remembered,

'moving furniture and arranging flowers'. Lytton Strachey staying there in 1918 described in a letter to Mary Hutchinson how he was conveyed to the castle 'in a tumble down dog cart', arriving to find 'everyone attired in evening dress, and tucking into a banquet of lobster and champagne'. He remembers it as, 'very dark, with nowhere to sit, and nothing but stone under, over and round you', but grants that the great foundations and massive battlements from which 'one has amazing prospects of the sea' are 'magnificent and extraordinarily romantic – on every side'.

The Congreves spent happy holidays with Edward Hudson at Lindisfarne. Lady Congreve wrote poems for the magazine and a photograph of her appeared as the frontispiece (now known as the 'Girls in Pearls' page). She described how her son Billy Congreve remembered Lindisfarne in his diary as, 'the most beautiful place he had ever seen – the castle that grew out of the rocks – and the happiest time of his life was passed there, because of the freedom and adventure'. Hudson used to send Billy

painfully shy and hated public life. Pamela Maude (her first husband was Billy Congreve killed after only ten days of marriage) noted his lugubrious looks, 'He was plain with a large head and long upper lip covered in a scrubby moustache. His arms hung at his side as though they were not needed'. Lytton Strachey described him as 'a pathetically dreary figure' and Ralph Edwards, the furniture historian, remembered him at the Country Life office,

With his close-cropped grey hair, rubicund counten-ance, fishy eyes and prodigiously long upper lip. Arrayed in a short black braided jacket, light waistcoat and striped trousers, when seated at his 'partner's desk' in the handsome boardroom, designed by Lutyens, intently scrutinizing the latest batch of proofs submitted for approval by his expert photographers he was the very picture of a prosperous British bourgeois, a typical minor Establishment figure.

One who remembered him with sympathy was Lutyens's daughter, Ursula, who was his god-daughter and described playing lions with him in the nursery and Christmas shopping. Christopher Hussey in his obituary of Hudson in *Country Life* wrote,

Edward Hudson had an extraordinary capacity for communicating his instinctive feeling to others, inspiring them with his ideals and guiding them with quick intuition.

He had robust health and untiring energy; he had a wonderful instinct which extended to his judgement of men as well as of beautiful things, and his friendship once given was life-long. Thus he gradually assembled round him a band of technical advisers and experts who helped him achieve *Country Life*'s high standard.

Although Hudson never wrote anything himself for the magazine he was a very shrewd businessman. At first the architectural side of *Country Life* was insignificant – a page and a half of print, two small photographs and one full page. Bernard Darwin recorded that, 'originally the houses

parcels to the front remembered with joy in his wartime diary, 'I got a parcel from that beloved Edward. Such a fine one too – a woolly jersey, a change of underclothes, a shirt, two pairs of socks, chocolate, and a box of those too much beloved Sullivan cigarettes'. Hudson had planned to give Lindisfarne Castle to Billy, but he died in action in 1916 (both father, Sir Walter Congreve, and his son serving in the Rifle Brigade won the Victoria Cross) and after the war Northumberland was deemed to be too far off and the castle was sold. A successor was eventually found for 'the dream castle' in Plumpton Place in Sussex, where Hudson, with Lutyens's help, repaired a romantic old manor house with a dreamy garden set on a string of lakes. The garden planning and planting was again by Jekyll. Hudson had long admired her natural planting, writing to her, 'I don't want what I call the *swagger* sort of gardening'. Hudson was in fact are treated in a more general and it may be said in a more amateurish way, than they came to be when Mr. Tipping began to write; the articles are neither so historically nor architecturally informed as they have long since become'. The genesis of these articles is interesting. Edward Hudson had a brother inclined to consumption and developed a habit of taking him on driving expeditions for the good of his health; the object of these trips was to look at notable houses, so country houses became Hudson's passion and

LEFT Lady Celia Congreve as photographed for the frontispiece of *Country Life*, 12 February 1916.

BELOW View of Plumpton Place in Sussex, restored in 1928 by Sir Edwin Lutyens for Edward Hudson.

this passion was shared with Tipping. Darwin recorded something of Tipping's persona at that period,

Mr. Tipping had been, I believe for some little time a don at Oxford, and something of this seat of learning hung about him in voice and manner. He had an essentially scholarly quality which permeated all that he wrote, and remained as a tradition in the accounts of country houses. Himself a trained historian, he was the first to apply the methods of historical research to the subject, and thus made an original contribution to biographical and architectural knowledge.

Ralph Edwards, his colleague at *Country Life*, added that Hudson regarded Tipping, 'as a veritable oracle'. Tipping,

'would burst into the boardroom like a tornado, and Hudson would instantly be transformed from a dictator to an obedient slave'. Of Tipping himself Edwards wrote, 'Blind in one eye, if anything put him out, he could, with the other, look very ferocious. He was of powerful physique and active mind, and genial (until crossed)'. Darwin added,

> He always seemed to me a distinguished visitant from another and more cloistered world, bringing a breath of academic air into a workaday London office. Yet nobody was more capable of dealing with the hustle and bustle of London; indeed, I retain one

BELOW Edward Hudson's Rolls-Royce, usually driven by Perkins the chauffeur and used by Tipping to visit country houses and gardens.

little vision of him treating it with a fine contempt. If he were walking on the southern side of the Strand and wanted to cross to Southampton Street, he would hold up his hand with an imperial gesture, bringing the traffic to a sudden and surprised stop while he sailed across with supreme dominion.

The *modus operandi* for writing country house articles was that initially Tipping went to visit the house, sometimes on his own, and sometimes meeting Hudson with his Rolls-Royce and Perkins the chauffeur, to ascertain whether it was worthy of inclusion in the magazine. This was particularly important during the war years when many properties had become hospitals or schools, or the garden had become run down. Then Tipping would return home to write the article, sometimes working at the London Library and British Museum to trace family lineage, and when the typescript had been sent to Hudson

for inspection, he would then send the photographer to take the images required. In May 1908 Tipping visited twenty properties in five days: Wingerworth Hall in Derbyshire (since demolished), Worksop Manor, Clumber (also demolished) and Newark Castle in Nottinghamshire, Southwell and Apethorpe in Lincolnshire, Southwick Hall, Lilford Hall, Broughton, Rushton Hall, Harrowden Hall, Stoke Bruerne, Easton Neston, Litchborough, Fawsley Hall and Edgecote in Northamptonshire, Farnborough Hall in Warwickshire, and on the last day Rousham, Studley Priory and Thame in Oxfordshire arriving back in London at 10.30 pm. The motor broke down for two hours and he had to miss Lyveden. The following week he worked at home and in the libraries and wrote seven articles for post by the Sunday. These articles appeared in the magazine over the next few weeks. In June 1908 he visited another twenty-two properties: Harleyford Manor in Buckinghamshire, Hartham Park in Wiltshire, Sutton Court, Halswell House, Poundisford Park and Lodge, Coker Court and Forde Abbey in Somerset, then Parnham House. He attempts to do Tollers (presumably Toller Porcorum) but fails and goes on to Athelhampton Hall in Dorset, then Moyle's Court, Boldre (for William Gilpin), Lyndhurst (for lunch) in Hampshire, followed by The Moot at Downton and Landford Manor in Wiltshire and then Stratton Park in Hampshire, followed by Cowdray House, Cooke's House at West Burton, Annesley Castle, Little Thakeham (Lutyens, 1903), Wiston Park and finally Rudyard Kipling's Batemans in Sussex. Altogether fifty-one articles by Tipping were published in 1908 in *Country Life*.

At Country Life Tipping was surrounded by people who shared his interests. One of the other early contributors and perhaps the most famous, was Gertrude Jekyll (1843–1932). In 1882 Canon Hole of Caunton, afterwards Dean Hole of Rochester and renowned rose grower, had introduced her to William Robinson and they became enthusiastic fellow workers, championing hardy plants, woodland gardens and popularising better ways of gardening. Jekyll met Hudson in 1899 and in turn introduced him to Lutyens. Her book *Wood and Garden* was reviewed in the March issue of that year. For

thirty years she contributed the main 'Garden Notes' to the magazine. Her articles were mainly about her garden at Munstead Wood but she also wrote about practical gardening and conservation. Tipping felt, 'she opened our eyes to the possibilities of the herbaceous border, of the woodland garden, of the bulb-set glade'. In spite of her weakening eyesight, she lifted gardening to the status of fine art with her talent for colour and form. One of Tipping's earliest articles for *Country Life* was on Millmead, built by Lutyens for Miss Jekyll.

Another contributor was Margaret Jourdain (1876–1951). She wrote intermittently from 1906 on the subject of antiques, an area representing potential advertising revenue for the magazine. Jourdain, a real bluestocking who had ambitions of a literary career, became highly respected as an authority on English furniture and interiors with 'few rivals and no superiors', as Ralph Edwards phrased it. Her job as saleroom correspondent for *Country Life* from 1922 was in fact her only salaried employment, but she had already worked for Francis Lenygon when he set up shop in Burlington Street before the firm became Morant & Co. She wrote *Decoration and Furniture of English Mansions during the Seventeenth and Eighteenth Centuries* under Lenygon's name in 1909 and *Decoration in England from 1666 to 1770*, a catalogue of the contents of the firm's Georgian premises in 1914. Jourdain did not seem to mind Lenygon taking the credit for the books she had written, even when this book was reviewed in *Old Furniture – A Magazine of Domestic Ornament*, 'Mr. Lenygon's writing is authoritive and the book is extremely well produced'. Perhaps she felt it was a fair exchange for all the specialist information he had given her. She also wrote *Decorative Arts in England* for Col. H.H. Mulliner and revised John C. Rogers's *English Furniture*. Her own pioneering book on William Kent did not appear until 1948. From 1919 she lived with the novelist Ivy Compton-Burnett and was known as a rather severe character with long skirts, feather boa, plumed hat and regency spyglass. James Lees-Milne recalls her, 'looking rather wicked and frightening when she looks through her quizzing glass', but he was one of the young men, along with museum curators, collectors and ambitious dealers and decorators,

LEFT Margaret Jourdain (right) taking tea with the novelist Ivy Compton-Burnett in 1942.
OPPOSITE LEFT Percy Macquoid on the beach at Hove, c.1920.
OPPOSITE RIGHT Ralph Edwards, who was on the editorial staff at *Country Life* from 1921 to 1926.

who sat at her feet to share her scholarship and acid wit. Tipping's Monday lunches with her at Edward Hudson's house in Queen Anne's Gate must have proved useful when he wrote *English Furniture of the Cabriole Period* in 1922, but he never acknowledged her.

Percy Macquoid (1852–1925), author of *A History of English Furniture* in four volumes published between 1904 and 1908, also contributed to *Country Life* from 1911 until his death. Tipping was an early neighbour in Ramsbury and a friend for forty years and greatly respected him for his knowledge of furniture, acknowledging his *History* as the work of a pioneer,

> Mr. Macquoid was the first serious student to bestow time and attention on a comprehensive study of the field, and to give the public the results of his labours. His volumes have maintained the premier place as a work of reference and instruction on English furniture.

Macquoid started out by designing costumes for a long list of plays produced at His Majesty's Theatre under the management of Sir Beerbohm Tree. Percy and his wife, Theresa, who were friends of most of the leading Edwardian actors and actresses, advised on 'period' interior decoration and built up a rich clientele in those circles. He was a notable connoisseur of old silver and furniture and in his own home in Bayswater, the Yellow House, built by George and Peto, each floor was devoted to a particular period of interesting furniture and beautiful pictures. The Macquoids also had a holiday house at Hoove Lea overlooking the sea at Hove. Edwards visited them there and recollected pottering around the Lanes with Percy looking for a bargain and 'visiting the fishmonger to obtain a red mullet and other marine delicacies of which Percy was very fond'. Percy was also an accomplished connoisseur of wine and 'when his tongue had been loosened by a few glasses of claret became a very agreeable and lively companion – even a witty one'. When Percy died in 1925, almost his last instruction for Theresa's guidance was, 'never give anyone a bad glass of wine'. At the time of his death he was working on *The Dictionary of English Furniture* with Ralph Edwards. When Theresa died, she bequeathed much of their valuable furniture and paintings to Preston Manor, a municipal museum on the outskirts of Brighton. Tipping wrote Percy's obituary in *Country Life*, appreciating his, ever-present kindliness, a sympathetic companionship about him, combined with a grasp of subjects such as decorative arts, painting, theatre as well as house and garden [mutual interests which they shared] and a fresh and humorous zest that made conversation or letter with him, ever agreeable.

Ralph Edwards (1894–1977), later to be Keeper of the Department of Woodwork in the Victoria and Albert Museum, was recruited by Tipping in 1921 also to write articles on furniture for *Country Life*. Edwards noted that he originally 'came into contact with Tipping through writing a laudatory review of the first volume of *English Homes*'. He added, 'Tipping was extremely susceptible to judicious flattery'. As Ralph Edwards explained, 'I was looking around for some congenial, and by the standards then obtaining sufficiently remunerative job'. Hudson

took him 'on the understanding that I should contribute articles, subsequently to form part of the raw material for Percy's [Macquoid] darling and long-cherished project for a *Dictionary*'. Macquoid agreed all the writing should be done by Edwards and eventually *The Dictionary of English Furniture* was published between 1924 and 1927 as a joint work of Macquoid and Edwards, with an introduction by Tipping. Macquoid died after the first volume, but Ralph Edwards completed the second and third volumes with Macquoid's widow Theresa, who had done much of her husband's research. Edwards also wrote many of the book reviews for *Country Life*. He was a devoted Welshman and spent much of his leisure in Monmouthshire, the county where Tipping was to spend his last forty years, creating houses and gardens. After 1926 when Ralph Edwards married, his annual boat race party at his home on Chiswick Mall (full of beautiful things) was a magnet for *Country*

Life contributors and Ralph Edwards's son in his memoirs remembers, 'Margaret Jourdain and Ivy Compton-Burnett attacking the fare provided with ruthless determination'. Ralph's obituary in *Apollo* in 1977 written by his old friend and publisher Denys Sutton records,

> Ralph was very much a figure of the eighteenth century; with his rakish hat and elegant cane he was rather a dandy. He could be irascible, but his friends realised that behind the mask was a man who cared for others. He was God fearing and upright, a Britisher of the old school.

Lawrence Weaver (1876–1930) joined the staff of *Country Life* in 1909, writing firstly about leadwork for Edward Hudson. His *English Leadwork – Its Art & History* had been published by Batsford in 1909. His interest was the small vernacular house and his contribution to the magazine was 'Lesser Country Houses of To-day', in which he championed the work of Arts and Crafts architects, particularly Lutyens and Robert Lorimer. Tipping wrote the first of the articles in this series on 'A house at Sapperton designed by Mr. Ernest Gimson' in March 1909, followed by 'A house at Sapperton designed by Mr. A. Ernest Barnsley' in April of that year. Weaver's publications for Country Life Library included *The House and its Equipment* in 1911, *Small Country Houses of To-day* in 1912, *Gardens for Small Country Houses* in 1912 (a collaboration with Gertrude Jekyll), *Houses and Gardens of E.L. Lutyens* and *The Country Life Book of Cottages costing from £150 to £600* both published in 1913. From 1910 to 1916 Lawrence Weaver was the general editor of the Country Life 'Library of Architecture'.

Country Life had its own highly profitable publishing company and published a series of finely illustrated and authoritative books. *In English Homes* in three volumes and edited by Tipping was described in the *Scotsman* as,

> A veritable revelation of the wealth of internal adornments, architectural and other, contained in the great country mansions of England. To turn over the pages is to obtain keen pleasure, as well as

enlightenment, concerning a treasury of domestic art and archaeology, which to a large extent is kept closed from the common eye.

The three volumes of *Gardens Old and New* were also edited by Tipping with photographs especially taken by Charles Latham. These were advertised as affording,

> a complete survey of the whole history of garden design and garden architecture, considered from every point of view, historical, artistic and horticultural.

Gertrude Jekyll's standard works, *Garden Ornament, Colour Schemes for the Flower Garden* and *Wall and Water Gardens* together with *Lilies for English Gardens* and *Children and Gardens*, were all published at the offices of Country Life. Gardening books such as *The Century Book of Gardening, Gardening for Beginners* and *Trees and Shrubs for English*

Gardens by E.T. Cook and books on the fruit garden, the unheated greenhouse, floral decoration, vegetables, seaside planting, carnations, pinks, violets, ferns and roses, were also published. *Causeries on English Pewter* by Antonio de Navarro, *Toys of Other Days* by Mrs Nevill Jackson, *Economies in Dairy Farming* by Ernest Mathews, *French Household Cooking* by Mrs Frances Keyzer and *Photography for Beginners* were also included in their list. There was also the Country Life 'Library of Sport' including cricket, fishing, shooting, golf and polo and the Country Life 'Series of Military Histories' for which Tipping wrote *The Story of The Royal Welsh Fusiliers* (see page 35).

The magazine was published every week on Thursday, in time for a new phenomenon – the weekend. Only since 2008 has publication day changed to Wednesday with the introduction of electronic publishing technology. At the beginning of the twentieth century, the developed railway system and the advent of the motor car, together with the increase in leisure time for many, meant that for the first time people could easily travel to the country. The professional classes had expanded hugely by 1900 and started commuting daily to escape the polluted atmosphere of the city, while some progressed to having a permanent second home in the country. Hudson was

LEFT Lawrence Weaver who wrote the series 'Lesser Country Houses of To-day' for *Country Life*.
BELOW Country Life stand showing Tipping's books and photographs from his series *English Homes*.

astute in that he glamorised the countryside and made the successful businessman long to live there, secure in the knowledge that by selling up and buying land he was on the first step towards becoming a gentleman. *Country Life* celebrated the virtues of vernacular architecture and pre-industrial handicraft within its pages. This accorded exactly with the tenets of the Arts and Crafts movement, which from William Morris's time had reacted against industrialism. Practitioners of the movement, C.R. Ashbee, W.R. Lethaby and Ernest Gimson, fled the cities and set up their own workshops in the Cotswolds. *Country Life* featured houses designed by the architects of the Arts and Crafts movement, particularly Edwin Lutyens. Lutyens close friendship with Jekyll was to lead to over a hundred collaborations before the First

World War. Her naturalistic planting softened his hard geometric lines. Hudson represented the view of so many of his readers. In her book on Lutyens Elizabeth Wilhide explains,

Hudson shared the same romantic view of the country as Lutyens's other prosperous upper-middle-class clients. The well-to-do businessmen and their families who formed the principal readership of the magazine could gaze week after week on lovingly photographed country houses and gardens and dream of building or buying their own. *Country Life*, as a record both of traditional houses and new houses built in the same spirit, served as the first 'lifestyle' magazine based on the virtues of domesticity and proximity to nature.

Country Life was significant in representing not only idealised country life, but also the romantic yearnings of the Edwardian period. The photographs of the tranquil interiors of these houses were often taken by Charles Latham (1847–1909), who created the magazine's tradition of country house photography. Hussey records that as early as 1903 Latham was denuding the rooms of country houses of their Victorian clutter and soft furnishings, presenting

LEFT Typesetters working in the print room of the Country Life building in Tavistock Street in 1919.
ABOVE A photograph by Charles Latham of the top of the garden stairway at Hutton in the Forest that appeared in *Gardens Old and New*.

instead, 'a few perfectly placed and apposite furnishings. Indeed one chair, placed askew in the foreground facing a fireplace, virtually became his signature.'

Latham first worked for *Country Life* in 1898 but was already recognised as an expert in the architectural photography field. He had taken the photographs for *The Architecture of the Renaissance in England* by J. Alfred Gotch (1891–94) and G.H. Birch's *London Churches of the 17th and 18th centuries* (1896), both published by B.T. Batsford. Latham, lame from birth, was remembered by Harry Batsford in *A Batsford Century* as 'a brilliant photographer'. His talent came with a red beard and entire absence of the letter H. Once he went to take photographs of a fine house which had been ruined inside by Victorian meddling. Latham hobbled into the room, stared round and said to

to 1957, and was used extensively by Tipping for his articles. He recorded, 'Mr Tipping says they object to some furniture etc. so much that they sometimes wait to photograph a house till it is empty changing hands'. Henson recorded in his diary that Tipping told him that Mr Evans had once waited at Exeter for three weeks to get one picture. Irascible, painstakingly slow, Henson was also completely single-minded and dedicated to his work of photographing country houses. Edward Hudson, with his expertise in printing, was heavily involved with the photographs, giving Henson notes indicating the viewpoints he wanted, as well as keeping expenses to a minimum, as is shown in this letter to Henson,

LEFT A photograph looking west along the south ambulatory at Westminster Abbey in 1911 by Frederick H. Evans.
BELOW Christopher Hussey (left) and A.E. Henson.
RIGHT A.E. Henson preparing to photograph the great hall at Rufford Old Hall, Lancashire, in 1929.

the owner, ''ateful and 'ideous. I'm glad I kept my cab.' Then he stomped out. The names of the photographers in the early days of *Country Life* were not recognised, but Latham's full appreciation came with the folios of *In English Homes* and then *Gardens Old and New* where his name is more celebrated than that of Tipping who was the editor.

Frederick Evans (1852–1943) was also commissioned by *Country Life* to take a series of images of the French chateaux in 1905. His evocative photographs of cathedrals also appeared in the magazine and in 1911 for the coronation of King George V, when Westminster Abbey had been stripped of everything movable to prepare for the ceremony, he was commissioned to photograph the abbey with its interior uncluttered and the mosaic floor seen in its entirety for the first time in centuries. Evans described the offer to take photographs for *Country Life* in 1905 as, 'a roving commission to [photograph] what I like, when I like, and how I like, so long as I give 'em of my artistic best'.

Later A.E. Henson (1885–1972) was the chief architectural photographer for forty years from 1917

20 Tavistock Street
Covent Garden,
W.C.2
June 1st, 1922.

Dear Mr. Henson,

Most certainly finish Wentworth Woodhouse and Seaton Delaval before you go on to Packwood. I will let you have the Seaton Delaval particulars immediately after the Whitsuntide holidays. I would suggest Castle Howard after Wentworth Woodhouse, as these houses are all in a group and it is no good paying travelling expenses twice over. Then, if you like you can do the Packwood gardens, but not the interiors, which can wait. Then I propose that you go to Bramshill, Hants; Cranborne Manor, Dorset and Longford Castle, Salisbury – these are all houses of the first importance. I do not think it matters whether Packwood is done now or in the Autumn. As far as I know, it is a yew hedge garden, something like Rous Lench, but not so good.

Yours faithfully,
Edward Hudson.

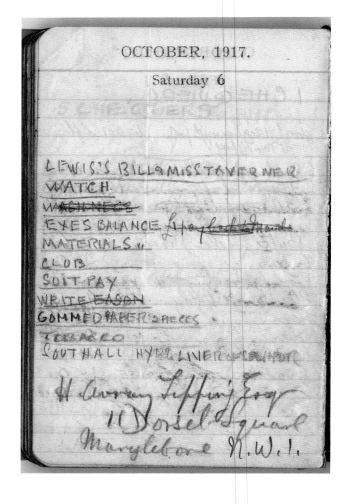

Alex Starkey, the *Country Life* photographer from 1952–88, recalled Henson's list of requirements demanded from the butler on arrival at a property. It included a very dry cellar (blackened out to make a darkroom), one table, one chair, one bucket, one empty gin bottle, one empty whisky bottle (so that developer and fixer could be indentified in the dark), a stepladder, white sheets etc. This ended with a request that he liked his tea at 4.30 pm with brown bread and butter. Henson always rigged up a darkroom so that he could develop his negatives on the spot to ensure they all reached his high standard. Much to the owner's annoyance and sometimes amusement, he insisted on lawns being cut a day or two before and in the right direction. Housemaids were dispatched to open windows, so the house did not look empty, branches of trees would be sawn off and once even a tree felled to give his camera a better view. Inside, like Latham, he insisted on rearranging furniture to avoid a room looking cluttered and owners and servants were

roped in to move quantities of chattels until Henson felt the scene would give him a well composed picture. He aimed at clear, diffused light with no black shadows and this often required black cloths to cover the windows, and yards of tissue paper. At one house he laid out all the looking glasses on the lawn to increase the light reflected into the rooms he was photographing. Lady Meade-Featherstonehaugh's account of Henson's visit to Uppark shows how exacting he could be,

complete with bowler hat on a lovely summer morning he stood in the Park waving a handkerchief – a signal that Lady Wolverton was to pull up the window blinds, which she was loath to do….and by his quiet kind insistence he had me and the butler and the chauffeur and my maid completely victimized, and he had a dark room rigged in 'Mr Weaver's closet'…and rigged so completely and in so short a time.

Henson left diaries and engagement books for the years 1916 to 1921. It was Tipping who suggested that Hudson should employ him after he had taken photographs of the garden at Mounton, as noted in Henson's engagement book for 31 July 1917,

> Mr Tipping told me when I said I thought perhaps he was the means by which I became connected with C.L. and that I ought to thank him he said Well yes I was.

Country Life agreed to engage Henson for a minimum of three years at a salary of £8. They provided all necessary apparatus and working materials and travelling expenses,

but Henson had to provide his own darkroom. There was a severe shortage of photographers during the war, and Henson as well as house visits, made a different kind of record, as at Wrotham Park in Middlesex, 'saw 2 fleet of German aeroplanes over London' and at Crowhurst Place in Surrey, 'gun firing all the time shaking things in the house' and 'constant exhaustion due to air raids causing lack of sleep'. Hudson kept the pressure on Henson, writing often urging him to finish a job and move on to another. His diaries record how he was travelling all over

LEFT Page from A.E. Henson's diary. Tipping has written his address at the bottom.
BELOW Letter to A.E. Henson from Edward Hudson requesting Henson's return from Ireland on 'special government business'.

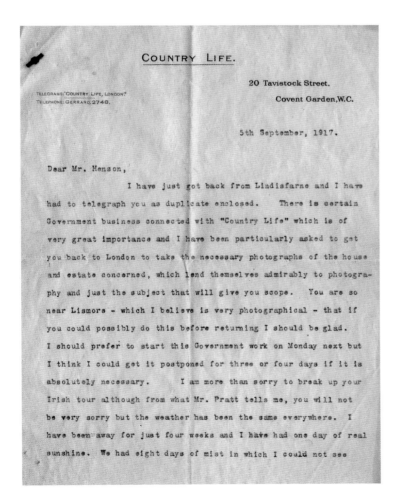

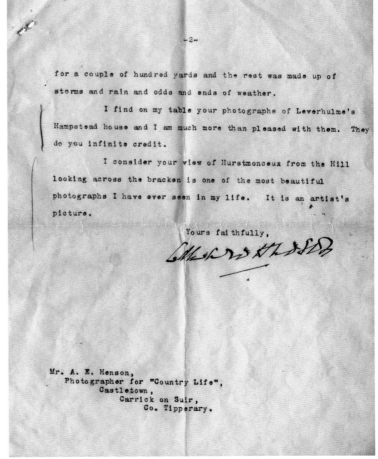

Britain, carrying heavy equipment. He had to juggle with interiors and exteriors depending upon the weather, as wind and light were critical. Often he worked a 12 hour day and had little time to spend with his family, and his diary shows some exasperation with *Country Life*, 'Mr Hudson has sent me a list of about a dozen houses in Ireland, 6 months work good to be done in 2 months'.

He was in Ireland in 1917 when he received a typewritten letter from Hudson calling him back immediately on 'Government business connected with *Country Life* of very great importance'. On Henson's return, worried that he might have to work abroad, he found the real reason, 'the job is at Sir. Arthur Lee's Chequers Court, Wendover Bucks' to accompany Tipping's articles on Chequers. All the papers contained the announcement that Chequers was to be handed over to the nation. Henson records on 4 October 1917,

> The secret is out first thing this morning. A *Daily Mail* photographer turned up and without any hesitation or waiting, he made exposures of the exterior in the rain and wind. Shortly after *The Times* and *Express* man calls.

Hudson's tight control of all aspects of the magazine showed in his manipulation of his photographers, and it is no surprise that *Country Life* has always been known for the quality of its photographs.

Through his writing and choice of accompanying photographs Tipping influenced the readers of *Country Life* by revealing the beauties of their own country, notably the great houses, their gardens and their contents. He also realised that the time was ripe to teach them because for the first time they wanted to be educated about domestic architecture and decorative arts. Roy Strong noted Tipping's comments on the treatment of country houses made on the occasion of the thousandth issue of the magazine,

> When the magazine was launched, the treatment of country houses had had to be 'tentative'. The ground was certainly fertile for a detailed consideration of them, he wrote, but, in a curious turn of phrase, one had to 'begin homoeopathically and only increase

the dose as the tonic gave strength to the reader's system'...'It has succeeded', he went on to say 'in being educative without being pedantic, informing yet attractive...each one has been so treated as to show some merit, teach some lesson, and exercise some influence on the taste of today.

Tipping had then proceeded to give a highly personal account of English architectural history, in which every period radiated glory, except for the Victorian era, when the country house was 'allowed to stray on to a very unsatisfactory line'. Harlaxton and Knebworth were held up as examples of, 'The extinction of a living style and an ignorant copying of every age and nation'. Tipping wrote that the aim of the articles was to give, 'hint and guidance to the many who propose to build or enlarge or re-do their habitations and their gardens'. These articles not only educated the public in good taste, but also supplied the history of the family as well as the house.

With the formation of the National Trust in 1895, stately homes were opening their doors to the general public. Tipping wrote many of the articles on National Trust properties and subsequently *The Story of Montacute and its House* and other such guidebooks. He was also a member of the Society for the Protection of Ancient Buildings, founded by William Morris in 1877, and brought its concerns for conservative restoration to a wider public. In this sense he is a seminal figure, translating the interests of academics and specialists into a medium attractive to the new middle class. It can also be argued that his pioneering work for *Country Life* laid the foundation of the whole 'heritage' industry and the vogue for country living and design.

Christopher Hussey (1899–1970) was Tipping's successor as architectural editor of *Country Life* and continued in his tradition. The Hussey and Tipping families had been friends in Kent for many years. Hussey was a committed journalist while still at Eton, writing *The Red Cross*, a collaboration with Ralph Dutton, a long-standing

LEFT Christopher Hussey in the library at Scotney, painted by his friend John Ward in 1964.

friend with close interests in architecture, country houses and gardens. His first contribution to *Country Life* was 'Public Schools on the Land' on 10 November 1917, following a request to the headmaster of Eton for an article written by a member of staff or boy on work done at harvest or other camps by public schools. Hussey was due to go to France on 18 September 1918 – but it was decided at the last minute that no new draft of officers was needed so he never went. His sister Barbara Birley remembers the armistice, 'This was marvellous for us but of course no one knew what to do next; owing to the war there had been no question of considering a possible future for any young man of his generation'. She was standing one evening in the drawing room at Hereford Road (the Husseys' London home) when suddenly Tipping swept up the stairs saying,

> I want that boy for *Country Life*. He must go at once to Oxford, try for a first and then he will come straight into *Country Life* – while he is there he can try his hand at articles during the vacation.

Tipping kept in touch with him while he was at Oxford and helped organise his first articles. The only letter from Tipping regarding Hussey's employment, dated 6 June 1920, set out the terms,

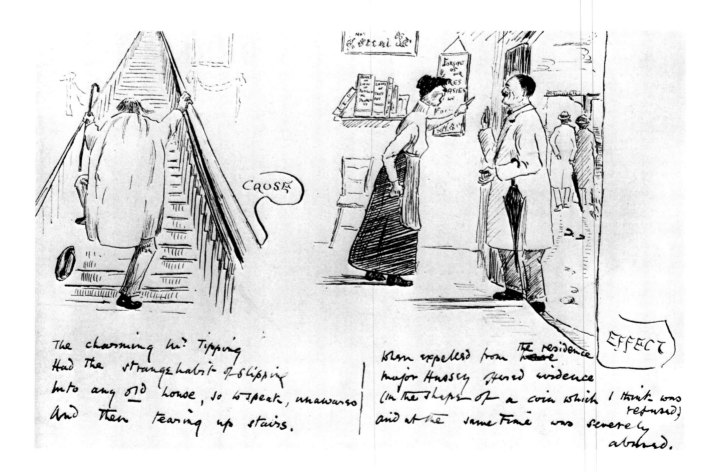

The charming M? Tipping
Had the strange habit of slipping
Into any old house, so to speak, unawares
And then tearing up stairs.

When expelled from the residence
major Hussey offered evidence
(in the shape of a coin which I think was refused)
and at the same time was severely abused.

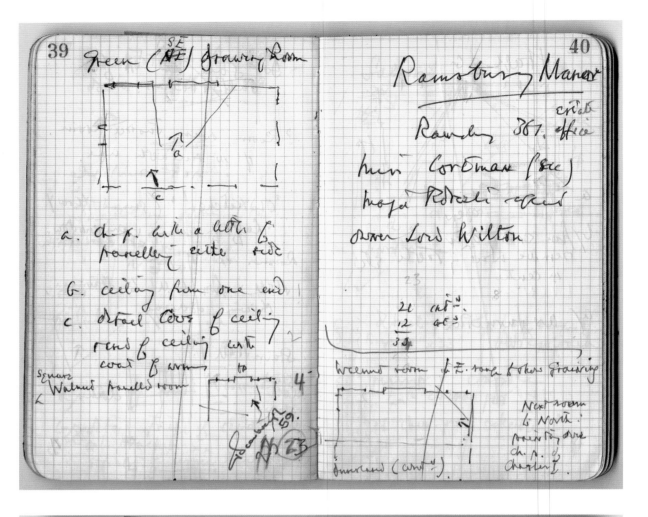

Green (SE) Drawing Room

a. ch. p. with a cloth &
panelling each side

b. ceiling from one end

c. detail Cove of ceiling
rend of ceiling with
coat of arms
Walnut panelled room
square

Ramsbury Manor

Ramsbury 381. office

Mrs Cortman (sec)

Major Rotseli open

owner Lord Wilton

21 int N.
12 at S.
33

Walnut room in E. range & then Drawing

Next room
to North:
painting over
ch. n. of
Charles I.

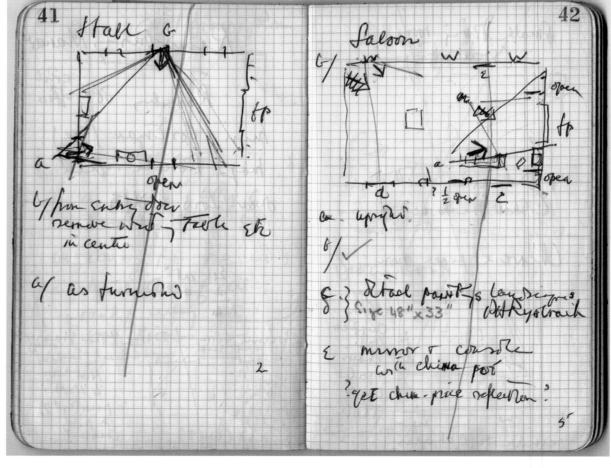

Hall G

b/ from ending door
remove wrdt g Table etc
in centre

c/ as furnished

Saloon

a. upright.

b/ ✓

c. } detail paint's landscapes
d } Size 48" x 33" Ot Ryotraih

e mirror & console
with china pot
? get chim.piece refraction?

5

My dear Christopher,

Country Life pays from 2 to 5 guineas per 1000 words and it would seem not out of the way for you, just at first to begin at the bottom, but I have arranged that you shall be on the 3 guinea scale. As a matter of fact, I am on that, but then the payment to me for contributions is really subsidiary to my editorial fee, and it is only because of the latter that I have never asked to be put down on the 5 guinea scale, which is an innovation due to present prices. Please note however that payment is inclusive and the contributors do not charge travelling expenses for visiting the places. That is why they are best arranged somewhat in districts or in the regions where the contributor lives or largely works, hence Mainwaring Johnson generally does Sussex, Herbert Kitchin, Hampshire, Gotch, Northamptonshire, only of late they have all been lazy and I have had to do nearly the whole thing.

Hussey was the heir to Scotney Castle in Kent where Tipping so admired the quarry garden and he shared with Tipping an absorbing passion for architecture, writing and the theatre. In April 1920 Hussey spent ten days at Scotney, writing his first three architectural articles, 'Scotney', 'Finchcocks' and 'Old Wilsey'. The only letter from Edward Hudson to Hussey (written in 1921) shows the close interest he took in every detail for his magazine, particularly anything to do with country houses,

> I should just make notes & plans of Rooms showing what you propose to Photo – keep them in Books –....I make plans of the Rooms – for house or Garden. With arrows showing what I want Photographed. Some of the arrow points I mark a b c d etc....I also note the furniture about the House & suggest moving it – to various rooms if necessary & I also note what they are *not* to bring into a picture.

Hussey's notebooks, held by the Country Life Picture Library, show how strictly he kept to these instructions when he revisited Ramsbury Manor in 1920. His

contributions to *Country Life* spanned fifty-two years. When he died in 1970 he had written nearly 1,500 articles excluding regular weekly leaders and other pieces bearing his *nom de plume* 'Curious Crowe, Tunbridge Wells'. He was an outstandingly prolific writer, also producing *The Picturesque* (1927), *The Life of Sir. Edwin Lutyens* (1950), *English Country Houses* (3 volumes 1955–58) as well as a wealth of other books, reviews, and country house guidebooks. His contribution to architectural scholarship is widely recognised by contemporary architectural historians. Sir John Summerson, Mark Girouard and Dorothy Stroud were all on the staff at *Country Life* under Hussey's aegis. Tipping did well to choose him.

Mr Walter Runciman, as president of the Board of Agriculture, once referred to *Country Life* as, 'keeper of the architectural conscience of the nation', but Hussey summed up the magazine on Hudson's death in 1936,

> For many years *Country Life*, and what it stands for, may be said to have been Edward Hudson's life, and it bore the stamp of his personality from the outset. It has never lost the character he stamped on it, and today it continues to be what it has been for many years, in someone else's phrase – 'a national institution'.

LEFT Hussey's notebook for his visit to Ramsbury Manor in 1920, showing plans of rooms with arrows for the photographer.
ABOVE Hussey's card which had to be signed by the house owner and returned to *Country Life*.

Mathern, Mounton and the Great War

I N 1894 Tipping bought some ruined buildings and land at Mathern near Chepstow. The old palace had been the chief residence of the Bishops of Llandaff from 1406 to 1706 but by the time Tipping arrived it was in a state of decay. What brought him to this much degraded medieval house in Monmouthshire, an area with which he had no family links, cannot be said in the absence of any surviving correspondence. Writing about Mathern Palace in *The Garden* in January 1900, Tipping explained what he had to work with,

> What remained of the old palace, after the lead had been stripped from the greater part of its roofs, and its interior woodwork and fittings had been destroyed or removed, was turned into a farmhouse. The gate-house, banqueting hall, and other now useless buildings provided material for barn and cowshed. The chapel was converted into a dairy, the kitchen into a stable.

Tipping records that John Leland had visited the palace in the sixteenth century and declared it to be a, 'pretty pyle in Base Venteland', although Bishop Pococke of Ossory (1704–65) did not agree and wrote in the notebook of his travels, 'it is but a mean building'. Archdeacon Coxe reveals that the buildings were already in a poor state a century before Tipping's purchase,

> The palace, which is a quadrangular building, inclosing a court yard, is now converted into a farm house, and is in a sad state of dilapidation; it still, however, preserves some remains of ancient grandeur, and from its irregularities has a picturesque effect. The outside ornaments of the eastern window of the chapel are still visible. The dilapidations

RIGHT Pencil sketch by G.H. Kitchin of the entrance front at Mathern Palace in 1909.

OVERLEAF The east front of Mathern Palace, Tipping's home for twenty years. This and the following black and white photographs of Mathern appeared in the *Country Life* article on Mathern in 1910.

Part of the Gate house.
Mathern Palace.
Aug 22 09.

have even extended to the library, which was once not inconsiderable. There now remains only a few worm-eaten volumes of the ancient fathers, without covers, and mouldering into dust.

Yet Mathern, seemingly beyond restoration, was the place Tipping chose to transform and make his own home for nearly twenty years, and that of his elderly widowed mother until her death in 1911.

Tipping faced a substantial task of renovation, repairing what could be saved according to the principles of SPAB, but also creating something for the present and future. He recorded in *English Gardens*,

Its amenities, therefore, were certainly not more than potential when I purchased it and set myself the task of making it habitable as a place of modern residence with as little serious interference as possible with its picturesque aspect and archaeological interest.

He also revealed his concern for conservation, 'Everything was overhauled and repaired, but this was done without any alteration of the general condition or interference with the patina of age'. The ruined refectory wall was left as it was and Tipping turned it into a high, narrow dining room. Tipping's friend G.H. Kitchin drew the new additions when he was staying there in 1899. From this room opened the outside loggia in which Tipping was photographed and which appears in many books on architecture of the period (see page 90). This is where he frequently took his meals outside, winter and summer, whenever the weather was favourable.

BELOW Aerial view of Mathern showing the kitchen garden with greenhouses and St Tewdric's Church.
RIGHT ABOVE The entrance front of Mathern Palace as it is today.
RIGHT BELOW The garden façade of Mathern Palace today.

Additions. Mathern Palace - 1899

The paved garden included the ruined walls and stone staircase of the old bishop's palace. He added a new conservatory with oak mullioning and leaded lights to harmonise with the surroundings. This was featured in Gertrude Jekyll's *Garden Ornament*. The west side of the quadrangle contained a building which was unsafe and, 'possessed no architectural feature whatever', so Tipping felt he had a free hand to add a gable to contain

LEFT The paved garden in 1910 showing the old ruined walls and stairs, with the loggia where Tipping took his meals 'in clement weather'.
ABOVE Pencil sketch of the new additions at Mathern in 1899 by G.H. Kitchin.
RIGHT Conservatory added at Mathern Palace and illustrated in the chapter on orangeries in *Garden Ornament* by Gertrude Jekyll and Christopher Hussey, first published in 1918.

a large L-shaped oak parlour. This room no longer exists in its original form, but Tipping had it carefully photographed for *Country Life* and it represents an ideal he cherished; an ideal to which he returned time and again in his houses. The mullion windows, beam and rafter ceiling, plain whitewashed walls and the careful placing of the old oak furniture are reminiscent of Hudson's hall at Deanery Garden by Lutyens. Kitchin drew the new room on a visit in 1900.

Tipping converted the shedding at the southern end into a flower room below and a gazebo or workroom above, lit on three sides by windows from which the garden could be viewed. On the north side of the west wing he repaired the gothic window with new tracery and added another narrow window to light the staircase he built inside. He admitted, 'this was an error' as it was competition for the restored gothic window and, 'it should have been plainly framed in unmoulded oak'.

This was separate accommodation for his mother, where she kept her own staff, horses, carriage, grooms and coachman.

Tipping took great care to add the usual domestic offices, 'in two little courts at the side of the building where they did not draw the eye away from the old work and the leading lines of its composition'. The name of the house implies a certain grandeur, but it only reflects its ecclesiastical origins and in fact Tipping transformed it into an unpretentious, romantic country home set in

LEFT The oak parlour at Mathern Palace in 1910. The corbels under the central beam show the Tipping crest.
BELOW Pencil sketch of the entrance to the new oak parlour by G.H. Kitchin in 1900.

a delightful garden. Tipping concludes his 1910 article for *Country Life*, 'It aims at being a quiet home where the simple life may be led' – in other words, Mathern was precisely the kind of place to which the readers of the new magazine were learning to aspire.

Tipping wrote about the gardens at Mathern Palace in his book *English Gardens*, 'So much for the house, which was and remained essentially old. Of gardens there was practically none. The sordid untidiness of a hopelessly ill-contrived and unrepaired farmstead prevailed.' He took special care not to lessen the appeal of the picturesque old building when he laid out the garden. In the quadrangle he designed a grass plat to fit into the ruins of the banqueting hall on the east, 'with a bed of dwarf evergreens, heaths and sedums (relieved by gladioli in the summer) which give some variety of form and colour in the winter at a point commanded by many windows'. Next to the door Tipping found, 'smothered with ivy, the live remnant of an old Banksian rose. No sooner had it regained its freedom than it shot forth, and in two years filled the thirty foot space from ground to roof and flowered profusely'.

LEFT The rebuilt wing from the northwest with the flower room below and Tipping's well lit workroom above.

RIGHT ABOVE The west side, with the old kitchen wing on the left, and the Banksian rose that grew thirty feet in two years.

RIGHT BELOW The yew arbour at the south end of the paved garden, with the view through it to the fields beyond forming 'a charming vignette'.

LEFT ABOVE Looking east from the garden shed to the rose arches, with topiary foxes and cock pheasants.
LEFT BELOW Looking west through the arches of rambler roses to the garden shed.
BELOW The bridge over the stream in the water garden made by canalising the medieval fishponds.

On the other side of the ruins, was another paved garden where Tipping planted yews to form an imposing circular yew arbour on the south. He was obviously pleased with the vista, remarking, 'along a flagged path, tulip bordered in spring, the view through it to the fields beyond forms a charming vignette'.

These upper terraces were bounded by low limestone dry-stone walls. Below this older enclosure, the sloping field was made into two grass terraces or bowling greens, linked by a cross axis contrived of a grass walk with cut yew hedges and topiary forms. Judith Tankard wrote in her book *Gardens of the Arts and Crafts Movement*, 'it was an enchanting garden, reflecting a distillation of the theories of Robinson and Jekyll'. David Ottewill in *The Edwardian Garden* described,

a grass walk, tulip-bordered in spring, was enclosed by a cut yew hedge sporting foxes, cocks and pheasants, almost mature when photographed for *Country Life* in 1910 after only ten years' growth.

LEFT Tipping's Christmas card for 1912, showing the Mathern Palace cricket team.

RIGHT ABOVE Tipping in *My Lord in Livery* at Chepstow Castle in 1898. Left to right: Norman Evill, Miss Annie Smith, Mrs Congreve, H.A. Tipping, Lancelot Francis (brother of Eric), Miss Rynd, Charles Evill. 'Mr. Tipping as Spiggott, an old family retainer, showed exceptionally high histrionic ability' according to the *Chepstow Weekly Advertiser*.

RIGHT BELOW Tipping and Celia Congreve at Mathern in 1904.

At its centre a cross path of yew ran east and west to a garden shed and tea house. The yew hedge was not extended on to the eastern boundary, but in its place, arches of rambler roses were created, separating two rectangular sunken gardens. Below the yew hedges Tipping planted Darwin tulips and forget-me-nots.

North of the house, the ground fell away to the old medieval fish ponds. Tipping made a terrace outside the gazebo and paths meandered through a rock garden to arrive at a bridge over the canal, which was formed by narrowing and lengthening the middle fish pond. On either side of the canal was a grass walk with aquatic plants along the waterside and herbaceous plants and bulbs on the outward, drier side as described by Tipping in *The Garden* in 1900,

> I stretched a broad grass path down it with a narrow boggy border for common Flags, Rushes, Forget-me-not, Mimulus, and other water-lovers on the canal side, and on the other side a wide gradually rising border, wet at the bottom, dry at the top, and so capable of satisfying the idiosyncrasies of plants with more or less thirsty habits. At the bottom, scarlet Lobelias, Japanese Flags, Rocky Mountain Columbines, Meadow-Sweets, Rudbeckias and the like flourish in large colonies.

The garden at Mathern is important as the first place where Tipping could give free rein to all his skills, from landscaping to the details of planting. In spite of the great deal of care which went into its construction, it is prized among his gardens for its informality. There were no grand pergolas, parterres and geometric gardens containing statues, as there were to be at his next home, Mounton House, only two miles away where he had also for some years been at work on water gardens in the valley.

These were happy, industrious days, spent gardening and writing with his dogs around him, his mother next door with her bath chair, his horse and carriage ready to take him to Chepstow station when summoned for another *Country Life* article. Like his brother at Brasted Place, Tipping kept a cricket ground for the villagers with his own Mathern Palace team, which he had photographed for his Christmas card in 1912. He entertained friends from Brasted, and was a regular visitor to Col. Curre at Itton Court, the Revd Robert Vaughan Hughes at Wyelands, Charles Edward Lewis at Moynes Court, George Carwardine Francis (the father of his architect at Mounton House and High Glanau) at St Tewdric, the Evills at Brynderwyn and the Stantons at Mathern House, all in the immediate vicinity of the palace. There were numerous house parties: the Scotts from Yews in the Lake District, Lady Limerick from Charlton, Mary Gwynne-Holford from Buckland and Celia

Congreve who acted in a play with Tipping at Chepstow Castle in 1899, Edward Hudson with Rolls-Royce and Perkins his chauffeur, and often for the weekend Oswald Eden Dickinson, his close friend who was the secretary of the Lunacy Commission. Peto and Kitchin were constant visitors planning houses and gardens together, with lunch parties and garden advice for Lord Rhondda at Llanwern House, sojourns to Tintern Abbey noted in Tipping's diary as, 'very beautiful with long shadows and sunlight' and even domestic duties, 'Freezing snow, put on pipes which won't work, so order new stove' and, 'arrival of new bath' and endless planting of shrubs, hedges and fruit trees. In 1912, after the deaths of his mother (aged 91) and the last of his brothers, Tipping sold Brasted Place and let Mathern Palace before putting it on the market. The 1914 sale particulars describe,

Wonderfully picturesque pleasure grounds comprise beautiful stone paved walks and a series of terraces, sunk Dutch gardens, long grass alley with walls of thick yew hedges, and cut yew ornamentals, old English garden, herbaceous borders, exquisite rock garden, tea house, dwarf stone walls, large level lawn for tennis, extremely picturesque water gardens with old fish ponds and long canal in the centre, crossed by rustic bridges, excellent kitchen gardens with glass houses heated by a furnace, the great garden house with men's rooms over for three men, and cottage.

The current occupiers, the British Steel Corporation, purchased Mathern in 1950 as a conference centre and it is still in their ownership. The gardens around the palace are still well kept up, but the yew hedges have grown so much that the cross paths have been lost and vistas to the house have disappeared. Instead of open axial grassways, they feel like enclosed dark paths, dramatically changing the atmosphere. The water gardens are very overgrown.

Through inheritance Tipping's personal wealth had much increased and he was able to start on his most ambitious building project, Mounton House near Chepstow, on a site above his water gardens, which had already been under way for five years. It was an opportunity not just to restore but to create. When Tipping arrived at the virgin site, he was a vibrant fifty-seven-year-old, bursting with the confidence of a lifetime's understanding of gardening, art and architecture, honed by the company of his stimulating circle of friends and acquaintances. His accumulation of knowledge would have far outstripped that of most of his contemporaries because it combined the academic and the practical. He

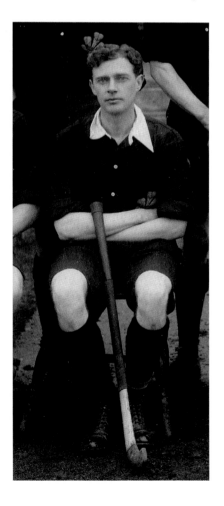

had taken architectural training, he had a keen knowledge of the historical aspects and domestic arrangements of houses and his planting palette was personal to him, adventurous and experimental. In his articles he agonised over the awful prospect of 'horticultural failure' should his plants fall victim to the altitude, the cold and the wind. In addition, he had the advantage of being both client and creator, without any constraints placed upon him by a previous architect or gardener. With no family to consider, for the first time he was free to express his interpretation of all he had learnt.

Mounton House was a collaboration between Tipping and a young Chepstow architect, Eric Carwardine Francis (1887–1976). In 1909 Francis was articled to Sir Guy Dawber, RA (1861–1938) and then became assistant to Detmar Blow (1867–1939). Dawber and Blow were both masters of the Arts and Crafts house. Dawber had been trained in Ernest George's office with Herbert Baker, Edwin Lutyens and Harold Peto. His speciality was creating Cotswold manor houses, almost indistinguishable from the real thing. Blow used to attend meetings at the Art Workers' Guild with Baker and Lutyens and worked with Ernest Gimson in Leicestershire and the Cotswolds. Francis developed his own Arts and Crafts style of domestic architecture and many distinguished buildings in Wales and the South West, including Wyndcliffe Court and East Cliff near Chepstow, and particularly his own home, Long Meadow at West Monkton in Somerset, remain as memorials to his particular flair for refinement in design.

The collaboration at Mounton brought together Francis's facility for unostentatious vernacular design and Tipping's learned taste. The house's architectural formality and the layout of the garden, displayed on a bare hilltop site, were a comprehensive expression of all Tipping's interests.

Mounton is his most important house and it was to be his home from 1912 to 1922. Tipping treated the flat site in a formal way, with the house approached through cottages, buttressed walls and outbuildings, at the end of a long park drive, similar to Markenfield Hall in Yorkshire (about which Tipping had written an article in *Country Life*). For the building, Tipping used local pink-stained limestone, much of it quarried on the estate, hammer-dressed into square blocks, and stone slates were used for the roofs. The forecourt was enclosed by a low wall in front and a higher one on the left, shutting off the service court, with a long single-storey building on the right, containing the long gallery. The entrance façade was defined by short gable-ended, stone-built wings returned on either side and a half-timbered section in between. The central section of the house had a projecting porch tower constructed in close-studding, in authentic fourteenth-century proportions. The oak and plaster were left in their natural colours, so that they were of even tone

with the stonework. Richard Haslam has written that Tipping, 'was too good a scholar to be misled into black-and-white'. John Newman, the author of *The Buildings of Wales: Gwent/Monmouthshire*, has proposed that the huge hipped roof above 'is surely an echo of Lutyens's Marsh Court in Hampshire'. The half-timbering, suggesting a late medieval house, was similar to that at Brinsop Court in Herefordshire, where Tipping had recently advised on the restoration (see pages 140–47). The chimneys rise along interior lines, so that, unlike so many of Lutyens's houses, the heat of fires is not wasted on outside walls. In the stone parts, the huge timber-framed windows are set under segmental relieving arches, similar to Moynes Court nearby. Tipping had beautifully crafted lead pipe-heads made for the house, moulded with his initials and even a Welsh dragon. Some are dated 1912, with a shield and flowers copied from one at Lydney Park in Gloucestershire. Tipping may have seen this in Lawrence Weaver's *English Leadwork – Its Art & History,* published by Country Life in 1909, or at the exhibition of leadwork at the Architectural Museum in Tufton Street in London held that same year.

The long garden front has three projecting gables, the end projections forming loggias, to the west columned and to the east with round-headed French windows. Between the gables the upper storey is hung with green Westmoreland slates. A stone terrace extends the full length of this façade. Entering the house, the ground floor divides into three main parts, each dominated by a principal room: the oak parlour, the dining room and the gallery.

OPPOSITE ABOVE Lead pipe-head with date and Tipping crest at Mounton.

OPPOSITE BELOW The entrance courtyard to Mounton House as it is now.

BELOW The garden façade of the house and terrace standing up from the bowling green.

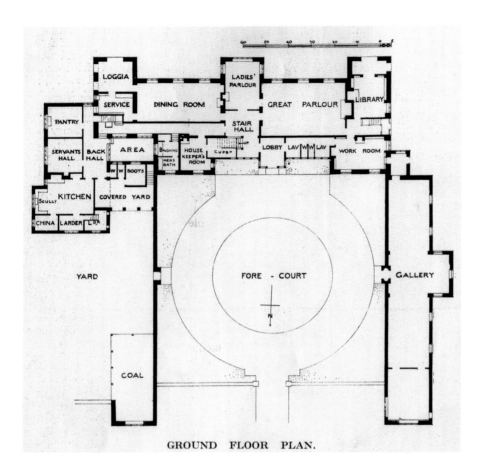

GROUND FLOOR PLAN.

LEFT The ground floor plan of Mounton House.

BELOW The great parlour, panelled in oak and showing the electric lighting of central lamps. The eight lights hanging from a wooden crown are almost smothered in tassels of coloured and knotted silk.

RIGHT ABOVE The long gallery, a single-storey wing, showing the Normandy armoires.

RIGHT BELOW The dining room with landscapes and portraits worked into the delicate plasterwork decoration.

The oak parlour, some 38 feet in length, is panelled in oak in heavy Jacobean style. This room is similar to the room from the Old Palace at Bromley by Bow, first displayed at the Victoria and Albert Museum in 1894. The moulded plaster ceiling is a copy of the ceiling of 1610–11 in Prince Henry's room over the Inner Temple gateway in London, the centre of which displays the Prince of Wales feathers and initials P H. The oak parlour differs in style from the dining room, which is decorated in an eighteenth-century style with Adam door-cases and a marble fireplace brought from the Tipping family home at Brasted in Kent. The long gallery is an independent single-storey wing. The style of the room was adapted to the collection of furniture that it was to contain, bought by Tipping's parents in France in 1865. It was dominated by three huge, eighteenth-century Normandy armoires. This room was designed for entertaining Tipping's guests and Martin Conway, who wrote about Mounton House in *Country Life* in 1915, noted, 'if in days to come great revelry goes on there it will not disturb the studious in the library or the weary in the bedrooms'. Upstairs, Tipping's bedroom was divided into two parts, separated by an open oak balustraded screen. John Cornforth wrote in *The Search*

LEFT Tipping's bedroom divided into two parts by an open balustraded screen, similar to the one at Brinsop Court, and a wagon ceiling of plasterwork copied from the gallery ceiling at Chastleton House in Oxfordshire.

RIGHT Tipping's workroom with inventive Arts and Crafts fireplace designed by E.C. Francis. Bound copies of *Country Life* can be seen on the shelves.

for a Style, 'the screen was surely inspired by one made by Lorimer for Earlshall' but Tipping had also restored a similar screen at Brinsop Court. The bedroom section had a coved ceiling of Jacobean style, with plasterwork copied from the gallery ceiling at Chastleton House in Oxfordshire. Tipping incorporated his own initials above the door. In Tipping's workroom, Francis designed an inventive Arts and Crafts chimneypiece with exposed brickwork and casts of Italian terracottas. Tipping was to copy this for a fireplace in the new wing at Weston Hall in Herefordshire for the Aldrich-Blake family.

The total cost of Mounton House was £40,000, earning it the local nickname 'Tipping's folly'. Tipping lived there in some splendour, entertaining peers, Cabinet ministers, including Lloyd George and Stanley Baldwin, famous figures from theatre and art connoisseurs to large and lavish weekend house parties. The garden, which was attended by twelve outdoor staff, attracted visitors from all over the world. This new gregariousness was in great contrast to his more simple life at Mathern Palace, although doubtless the presence of his elderly mother at Mathern had been an influence.

Today the main house and outbuildings have been developed into flats. The oak parlour and dining room still exist in their original state, but the long gallery has been divided.

The complex of gardens at Mounton, created between 1907 and 1912, shows that Tipping was a passionate and knowledgeable gardener. The two most obvious influences on him were William Robinson and Gertrude Jekyll. These two giants were the catalyst for a major change in the design of the English garden, departing from the formal parterres and garish bedding-out so popular in the Victorian era. Robinson favoured the laying out of gardens as part of the natural landscape and vigorously attacked Reginald Blomfield's book, *The Formal Garden in England*, published in 1892, as well as J.D. Sedding's *Garden-Craft Old and New*, written the previous year. Jekyll, Tipping's friend and associate at *Country Life*, weighed up both sides of the controversy in the *Edinburgh Review* in 1896 and concluded, 'Both are right, and both are wrong'. Tipping concurred,

The old school of formalists aimed at banishing Nature, just as the late landscapists sought to banish formalism. Our best schools of to-day rightly insist upon combining the two.

Tipping had read Robinson's books, *The English Flower Garden* (1883) and *The Wild Garden* (1870). He would also have read Gertrude Jekyll's first book, *Wood and Garden*, published in 1889 and *Wall and Water Gardens*, which followed in 1901. Jekyll was writing 'Garden Notes' for *Country Life* at the same time as Tipping was dominating the architectural writing for the magazine. She must have had a considerable influence and it has to be possible that she was consulted on the planting at Mounton.

Tipping took equal care over the design both of the natural garden and of the formal garden. 'The best of gardening', he wrote in 1900, 'is perhaps to lovingly tend one of nature's choice spots, to remove what injures, and to heighten what improves its form, to vary and stimulate its flora, to retain the grace and feeling of the wild, while adding the eclectic richness and reasoned beauty of the cultured'. He certainly put this into effect in 1907 when he created the natural water garden in the gorge at Mounton.

Perhaps Tipping's most important contribution was that he carried the mantle of Robinson and Jekyll into a new century, as noted by Christopher Hussey who wrote,

As a young man he was one of that small band of followers that gathered round Mr. Robinson and Miss Jekyll in their crusade for natural planting against the wearisome 'bedding out' practised in the seventies and eighties. But in the long campaign between the advocates of the wild and the revived formal garden – the latter led by Sir Reginald Blomfield – he adopted, from the first, that middle course which common sense dictated and which has become the accepted view today.

Tipping's garden designs all have the added dimension of exuberant planting, planned to provide huge splashes of colour at all seasons of the year. Lady Congreve wrote that 'he was like Kipling's artist in *When Earth's Last Picture is Painted* who in Heaven was going to "splash at a ten-league of canvas with brushes of comet's hair"'. For Tipping the designing of gardens was definitely an art form.

It is all too easy to condemn Tipping as just a follower. Rather he should be seen as 'school of', a student who had finished his studies by the time he left Mathern and who proceeded to express his own personal vision within the modern movement in gardening. Tim Richardson in *English Gardens in the Twentieth Century* wrote that Tipping, 'displayed a confident handling of formal features such as terraces and enclosed rose gardens, allowing them to segue together with more informal elements of the garden'. In his gardens one may see a glimpse of Munstead Wood, Deanery Garden, Hestercombe and Rodmarton, but although he may

have been influenced by William Robinson, Gertrude Jekyll, Edwin Lutyens, Harold Peto and Ernest Barnsley, his gardens were his own creations, always dovetailing the house and garden as a unit.

The most influential garden in this period was Jekyll's own garden at Munstead Wood. Jekyll was creating the woodland gardens there from 1883, although the house by Lutyens was not built until 1897. Jekyll established a number of ornamental gardens devoted to flowers of one season, as she explained and illustrated in *Colour in the Flower Garden* in 1908. Frances Jekyll, in *Gertrude Jekyll – a Memoir*, wrote, 'Mr H. Avray Tipping was among her visitors in 1909', but he had already visited Munstead several times. In 1908 after visiting Orchards, a house designed by Lutyens for Julia Chance, Tipping soaked by the rain, took tea with Miss Jekyll and enjoyed the warmth of her workroom fire. Tipping was later to include a chapter on Munstead Wood in his book *English Gardens* written in 1925. He wrote,

BELOW Gertrude Jekyll's workroom fireplace at Munstead Wood, drawn by G.H. Kitchin in 1907. Tipping enjoyed 'tea and warmth' there after a wet visit to Orchards in 1908.

Miss Jekyll…as an editor of *The Garden*, as a contributor to other journals and as a writer of standard and much-consulted books, has taught us right principles and improved practice in garden making, planting and cultivation.

He admired her herbaceous borders with their large drifts of irises, lupins and peonies and felt her greatest contribution to gardening was her mature understanding of plants and colour. Gertrude Jekyll designed over four hundred gardens and even today her methods endure in the way we arrange our gardens and borders, in our use of colour and the way we use plants to soften the hard lines of garden architecture. Tipping certainly used plants in the same way as Jekyll in the formal gardens at Mounton. He specifically used her own selections of *Aquilegia* 'Munstead White' and *Nigella* 'Miss Jekyll Blue' and *Nigella* 'Miss Jekyll Dark Blue' in his gardens.

Two more important and influential gardens of the Jekyll Lutyens partnership, were Deanery Garden (1901) for Edward Hudson and Hestercombe (1908) for the Portman family. Judith Tankard has stated, 'the formal terraces around the house at Mounton rivalled those at Deanery Garden [by Lutyens] in ingenuity and visual appeal'. An additional influential garden must have been Gravetye in Sussex, created from 1884 by William Robinson, whom Tipping called, 'our horticultural *doyen*, the senior alderman

BELOW The pansy garden at Munstead Wood by Thomas H. Hunn. Tipping much admired Jekyll's 'gay borders' in his chapter on Munstead Wood in *English Gardens*.
RIGHT Gravetye Manor, the home of William Robinson, looking down on the house and garden from the bowling green today.

of our gardening corporation'. In 1911 he published *Gravetye Manor, or Twenty Years' Work round an Old Manor House* and it was here that Robinson gave his most convincing testimony to wild gardening. Rodmarton Manor, designed by Edward Barnsley in 1909 for the Biddulph family, was another example of a true Arts and Crafts garden. The garden was a series of outdoor 'rooms', with a terrace, trough garden and topiary and long herbaceous borders, culminating in a stone summerhouse.

Tipping wrote in his diary on 9 September 1912, 'pavement laying and other garden work in progress', followed six weeks later by the entry, 'pergola garden being planted and dry wall beginning'. This period saw the inception of most of the formal garden at Mounton House, although the yew hedges and the construction of the rocky bank below them and the bowling green, had been started earlier. The gardens are composed of two

separate regions; the natural wood and water garden, created in the limestone gorge below the house five years earlier, and the contrasting formal garden around the house, on the plateau above. Tipping made a sketch plan of the formal garden for his book *English Gardens* published in 1925.

The gardens began with a flagged terrace next to the house, above the long grass bowling green surrounded on three sides by clipped yew hedges.

Tipping planted pomegranates and myrtles, magnolias and Edwardsias and *Solanum jasminoides* and *Solanum crispum* against the house wall of the terrace. He often experimented with plants not used before in certain situations. In 1917 he recorded,

Against the house were set a variety of climbers and wall shrubs, all of which did well till last winter

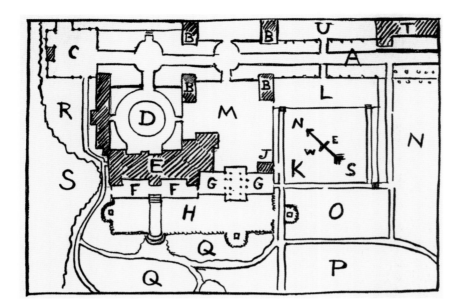

LEFT Tipping's plan of house and formal gardens at Mounton.

A The drive between buttressed walls
B Gable ends of garage and outbuildings
C Colonnade D Forecourt E House
F Terrace G Pergola garden
H Bowling green J Tea house K Lawn
L Parterre M Kitchen court
N Tennis court O Shrub bank
P Tree planted rough ground
Q Rock garden R West garden
S Precipitous descent to water garden
T Cottages U Kitchen garden

taught them the rigours of life. Clianthus puniceus was done to death and of veronicas all the speciosa hybrids succumbed.

In between the projecting gables on the terrace were sheltered paved areas for sitting out on windy days. At each end of the terrace protruding coped walls, pierced by arched doorways, gave a feeling of shelter and seclusion. The doorways gave enticing views to what lay beyond. The pergola garden and dining loggia are on the southeast and the steep precipice to the gorge to the northwest.

The view from the terrace was of the River Severn with the hazy Mendip Hills beyond. It was little changed from a century earlier, when the Romantics celebrated the same landscape. From the centre of the terrace, a broad flight of steps led down to the bowling green, surrounded by yew hedging. At either end of the bowling green, in front of a circle of yew, Tipping set the huge urns that he brought with him from Brasted Place his childhood home.

LEFT Urn from Brasted Place in Kent, placed at the end of the bowling green at Mounton.

RIGHT The steep rock garden below the bowling green, but above the precipitous descent to the water garden.

Through the doorway, at the southeast end of the terrace, there were three steps down into the pergola garden that stretched beyond the house. A rectangular lily pool occupied the centre of the stone pergola, comprising an astonishing twenty-four pillars. In the centre of the pool stood a water-spouting boy on a column surrounded by water lilies. This statue, a copy from Pompeii, is exactly the same as the one in the pool on the garden front at Deanery Garden. The pergola was planted with roses, 'American Pillar' and 'Dorothy Perkins', 'Lady Gay' and 'Dorothy Dennison' and wisteria.

Gertrude Jekyll was impressed by the Mounton pergola, using it as an illustration in her book *Garden Ornament* (1918). She noted, 'Mr Avray Tipping's pergola at Mounton or Mr Robinson's structures at Gravetye depend for their effect on a luxuriant overgrowth'. She also visited the water garden, as Sally Festing recorded in *Gertrude Jekyll*,

> She had visited places like Avray Tipping's water garden at Mounton in Monmouthshire, a rocky limestone gorge with sheer cliffs and steep tree-clad hangers that showed him to be a true disciple of nature.

ABOVE The paved terrace at Mounton, seen through the projecting coped wall pierced by an arched doorway.
RIGHT The central alley of the pergola garden.

Tipping drew a plan of the pergola in his last book *The Garden of To-day*. He described it as,

opening from the dining-loggia (A) with arches opening west on to a terrace (B) but south into a privy garden with three sides enclosed by buildings or high walls, the fourth or west side being a parapeted terrace wall raising the little garden up from the lawn (H) and giving a wide prospect. The pergola (D) occupies the central portion, its length being the breadth of the privy garden increased by bays. The western bay stretches out into the lawn from which, there being four feet of retaining wall, the pergola piers rise fourteen feet. From the level of the privy garden they rise ten feet, by no means too much to sustain the rafter arrangement on which the rambler roses and Japanese wisterias lie. Supported by the ten foot east wall the pergola forms a sort of open cloister with paved walks and flower-beds on each side of it, while the centre is shaped as a broad paved way framing an oblong pool (E) in the centre of which a water-spouting bronze boy stands on a short column that rises from the lily-decked surface of the pool.

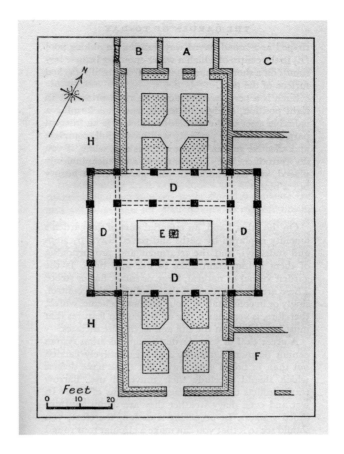

Tipping's pergola garden at Mounton was certainly one of the most impressive pergolas of the Arts and Crafts period, not only for its size, but for its exuberant planting. The only pergola similar in layout was perhaps at the Villa Rosemary in the Alpes Maritimes, laid out by Peto in 1910–11 (see page 40).

Tipping wrote in 1917 in *Country Life* that, 'the parapet wall that runs along the open side of the pergola garden is seen altogether bosomed with Dorothy Perkins and Lady Gay, which at this height escape mildew and grow riotously'. The surrounding formal beds, 'appear in May, when tall Darwin tulips sway in the wind. When rose-time comes round they are mauve with Maggie Mott violas'. A statue of the goddess Diana stood in a circle of clipped yew on the bowling green below the end of the pergola. This statue and the others in the *Country Life* photographs taken by A.E. Henson in 1916 are no longer there.

From the pergola garden it was possible to pass out to the lawn, either through the door or through an open-sided two-storey tea house. Martin Conway described the tea house as, 'a garden house overlooking the croquet lawn, which, facing east, provides a shady sitting-room below and sleeping-out loggia above'. The parterre, as Tipping called it, above the lawn was surrounded by tall stone walls and Lady Congreve remembered being shown round the garden with her husband,

'That wall must have cost you a pretty penny, Harry,' said my husband. 'Yes' said Harry in his most incisive way. 'You see, I do not care to keep racehorses or dancing ladies. I prefer to spend my money on walls.'

LEFT The water-spouting boy on a column rising out of the rectangular lily pool in the pergola garden.

ABOVE Tipping's plan of the pergola drawn in *The Garden of To-day*.

In June there was a show of peonies in the parterre and, later in the season, a display of *Aster thomsonii*, one of Tipping's favourite flowers. He used great drifts of the same flower, in the way advocated by Jekyll, to soften the geometric stonework. To the west of the house, on the edge of the gorge, there was a colonnaded garden with statues overlooking the valley below. Again this was filled with Darwin tulips in springtime.

From the formal gardens around the house and below the bowling green, a rock garden and ponds were set in a wilder area, leading to the woodland and water garden below. This area of semi-natural woodland was planted with mixed deciduous and coniferous trees. There were viewing platforms and winding paths among the natural rock formation to the bottom of the valley and the water gardens. Tipping had bought a small farm called Mounton Dene and some land at the foot of the Mounton gorge in 1907 some five years before he built Mounton House and he had constructed a water garden in natural style around the winding stream. The plan was published in *Country Life* in 1910.

The shed (shown in the plan) was a sleeping hut as noted in his diary on 30 July 1908, 'To Mounton to try sleeping shed – warm foggy night and very pleasant out'. From then on he regularly walked down to Mounton in the evening and in August he wrote, 'open air sleeping all week'. His friend Kitchin drew Tipping sitting outside the sleeping hut in 1906.

He repaired the tumbled down cottages, writing two pages about their renovation in *Country Life* in 1908 explaining,

The extreme picturesqueness of the limestone gorge led me to convert into a wild and water garden the end

of the farm which lay within it, and which consisted of a steep hanging wood, studded with fine indigenous yew trees rising out of the rocky clefts, and of a diminutive flat meadow through which danced the clear stream. Here two of the most neglected cottages constantly caught the eye and spoilt the picture.

He bought and renovated 'Wests' cottage for the gardener and 'Joneses' for himself, noting in his diary that he often took his guests for meals there or to stay in the summer,

I arranged [Joneses] as holiday quarters for any friend who likes summer picnicking amid beautiful surroundings such as this valley offers. I therefore added

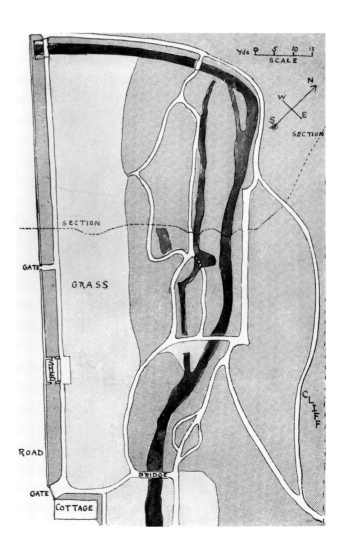

LEFT ABOVE The house and its environing walls showing the parterre planted with *Aster thomsonii* and the tea house.

LEFT BELOW The west garden planted with Darwin tulips set on a narrow plat on the edge of the precipice.

RIGHT Tipping's plan, illustrated in *Country Life* in 1910, of part of the water gardens in the Mounton Valley. Tipping called this 'the work of his leisure moments'.

ABOVE 'Joneses' cottage (left) as sketched by G.H. Kitchin before Tipping's restoration in 1908, 'with chimney toppling, tiles off or awry, windows broken, woodwork decayed and a surrounding of scattered potsherds instead of trim gardens' and (right) after restoration. Tipping spent £75 on its improvements.

LEFT Pencil sketch of Tipping sitting in the stone shelter in the Mounton water gardens by G.H. Kitchin in 1906.

no rooms, and there are only two bedrooms. I removed the ruinous and leaky roof-windows, which were so low as merely to light your boots, and put new ones at a convenient level in the gable ends. This gave me an unbroken sweep of roof, which I brought down over the doorway as a porch and over the bay window, which I added to give sunshine and gaiety to the living room.

In many ways this natural garden was more successful than the formal garden above. In an article in *Country Life* in 1910, Tipping described how carefully he supervised the artificial stream bed so that the water was under command and the curves, levels and contours resembled those of nature as closely as possible. The zigzag paths were laid with rough limestone paving from a neighbouring quarry. Tipping recorded,

> The water was let in from the natural to the artificial stream-bed through a pipe in the bank, which can be closed, half opened or fully opened at will. The water is made to look, at its entry, as if it bubbled up amid great stones from a spring. It then dances rapidly down over stones and round corners until it reaches a wider and more level portion of the bed, where it lies placidly, and is crossed by stepping stones.

He recorded in the one diary we have, 'bought railway to help with earth moving' and 'men laying water pipes' and finally, 'to water works where excavating and pipe laying go merrily'. Away from the stream Tipping set flowering shrubs: 'lilacs, Japanese guelder roses, Judas trees, weigelas, deutzias and philadelphias'. Tall perennials, rudbeckias, anemones and phlox were grouped beyond these. The stream bed was set with moisture-loving plants such as gunnera and rodgersia, while New Zealand flax and Siberian irises grew alongside. The water gardens in this peaceful valley still partly exist, but the cottages have now been extended.

The garden at Mounton was a testament to Tipping's passion for gardens, with every detail carefully pondered and executed. It is a garden of strong structural bones but where the atmosphere was defined by relaxed and luxuriant planting. Only a designer with a sure understanding of both plants and structural aspects of gardening could have achieved a garden of such beauty. In 1922 Tipping handed over Mounton to his late brother's godson, Hubert Capel Loft Holden. The Holden family remained at Mounton until 1935 when the house was sold to Mrs G.R. Liddell of Lydney Park, Lydney. In 1946 Mrs Liddell sold the property to Mr John H. Watts of Lydney, who conveyed it to John Watts Hotel Ltd in 1947 and in the same year to the National Provincial Bank Ltd. In 1948 Mounton House was bought by the Trustees of the Royal Cambrian Residential School for the Deaf and in 1951 sold to Monmouthshire County Council who used it as a special school for handicapped children. The house and part of the land was sold in 2002 to developers and has been converted into approximately thirty flats and cottages.

Tipping had inherited an interest in social questions from his father and in 1874, just before going up to Oxford, he had visited the great cooperative community of La Familistère de Guise, founded by Jean-Baptiste Godin. The outbreak of the First World War sharpened his concern to improve the living conditions and health of the general population. Edward Hudson had pledged Country Life's resources to the war effort within a fortnight of the declaration of war. The issue of 15 August 1914 called on the upper classes, 'to live sparingly' and articles followed on sending horses from the hunting field to the front, collecting wild fruits in the hedgerows and increasing food supply on farms and in gardens. The big landowners released all their estate workers for the war in a great surge of patriotism, country houses were turned into hospitals and women, including duchesses, their servants and housewives left at home, were photographed in nurses' uniforms, labouring on the land, mending roads and working in munitions factories. The shortage of staff in the office meant that Tipping turned his hand to a variety of war-related articles as well as his usual writing on country houses and gardens. His 'Feeding the children' in June 1915 encouraged the use of village institutes to provide penny dinners for school children in rural areas. He gave the example of Lady Aberconway in Eglwys Fach, detailing her menu for the first week in May:

May 3.   Ox head Soup: Baked currant and raisin pudding.

May 4.   Irish stew: Rice, currants and raisins.

May 5.   Marrow-bone soup: Baked butter-milk and raisin pudding.

May 6.   Sheep's head broth: Boiled jam roley.

May 7.   Sheep's head pie: Rice, rhubarb and currant pudding.

The sixty-one children paid 4d. a week for these wholesome home-cooked meals with 'bone-forming ingredients' and he urged the importance of fitness and feeding children in a country training for war.

He also wrote of the need for women to work on the land after it became clear that every man under forty-one would be called up for national service, leaving farmers with insufficient labour. One of his own gardeners at Mounton, Miss Thorne, who had practical working knowledge of farm routine, raised a group of forty local women to work part-time. The first task was, 'weeding a ten-acre field of autumn-sown wheat which was moderately foul with thistles and docks' but eventually the work became more varied and girls who were free for the whole week were employed as garden assistants, to release old men and boys to give a hand with the hay. Pay was fixed at only 3d. an hour, 'little compared to what women are getting in towns', but Tipping pointed out that most women in the group were wives and daughters of well paid men so, 'The work, then, is not undertaken from personal necessity, but rather as a patriotic duty', noting also that, 'it brings together for a useful and national purpose women of various classes and aptitudes', cooperating 'cheerfully and effectively'. He added that one of the main problems was getting farmers to acknowledge that the scarcity of male labour was intensifying and that the busy time of hay-making and harvest could only be met by accepting the work of women.

Tipping let Mathern Palace as a home for twenty-five Belgian refugees and contributed generously to war charities. He provided material for the people of Mathern and Mounton to make shirts for the Chepstow Company of Territorials, away on service. He made public speeches to raise the standards of local horticulture, combat unemployment and improve town planning. In fact he was deeply interested in well designed and well arranged housing for all levels of society. He had already experimented with cottage building on a farm near Chepstow, as was illustrated in The 'Country Life' Book of Cottages.

In 1913 Tipping was asked to takes shares in, and a seat on the board of, the Housing Reform Company at Rhiwbina on the east side of Cardiff. He was a keen supporter of this garden village from its inception and believed the company had, 'found a solution to the jerry-building difficulty, which would altogether disappear when the people declined to live in jerry-built houses, just as they would decline to live in pig-sties'. Tipping firmly approved of the ideals of the Garden Village Society 'to promote the health and happiness of its members by enabling them to live a country life in close proximity to their work'. The architect was A.H. Mottram, on a layout by Raymond Unwin, who had already worked at Bournville, Letchworth and Hampstead. Each resident held shares and had a voice in the running of the society. All the houses were built with electric light, gas heating and were separated by beech hedging. There were different styles of house, ranging from 7 shillings to 11 shillings and 3 pence a week rental. The Rhiwbina project was very difficult, owing to lack of financial support, but Lord Davies and his sisters from Gregynog helped and Tipping became the society's largest single investor, making a substantial interest free loan of £11,000. His obvious frustration with other pillars of the community was expressed in a letter to the Western Mail on 23 September 1913, 'Cardiff takes the lead in the ample and stately placing of splendid public buildings, but she is at present at the tail end in the matter of her suburbs, those dreary wastes of brick and mortar where her clerks and operatives spend their home life' and it struck him, 'as peculiar… that the movement [Rhiwbina Garden Village] had not caught the attention of wealthy men at the head of the prosperous Cardiff community to the extent of their giving it financial support'. He purchased land between the

LEFT The stepping stones across the artificial stream in the Mounton water gardens with the sheer cliff face above.

existing houses at Rhiwbina and the railway and set about building eighteen houses at Pen-y-dre (known as Homfray Road) with his own architect, Eric Francis. Tipping chose to curve his road along a natural stream with the cottages set back on one side of the road, with a small wooden bridge over the stream for each, creating a uniquely picturesque effect. He always felt, 'delightful as the formal pool may be, as a garden amenity, the running brook surpasses it, whether we have it by nature's gift or create it in imitation of her'. The society acquired these houses

at the end of the war and Tipping waived monies owed to him, enabling these funds to be used to create a cricket ground and recreation hall. Shops, churches, a tea house (representing the temperance mood of the garden city theorists) and a library were built to meet the needs of the growing village and in 1922 Tipping opened the new hall where activities included a horticultural society, reading club, choir, dance classes and camera club. After Tipping's death, Walter Ernest Wood inherited the mortgage, but gave up the interest, turning it into the Tipping Fund to

LEFT Advertisement with its slogan 'Health for the Child' expressing the ideals of the 'Rhubina' Garden Village Society.
RIGHT Tipping opening the Recreation Hall at Rhiwbina Garden Suburb in 1922.

be spent on open spaces, tree planting, hedges and seats around the cricket field. It is now a conservation area.

Tipping was also interested in schemes to salvage the Chepstow shipyards when these became the object of government support in 1917. Chepstow was to become 'A City of Ships' and the military acquired the Beachley estate to develop the area into an important naval and shipbuilding centre. The villagers were given 14 days notice to leave and were forced to take a patriotic view of the acquisition of their village. The Standard Yard Company proposed a large garden city on the higher part of the town, but the scheme never materialised when the Admiralty commandeered the Standard Yard. The government scheme meant an influx of military and conscript labour, and the housing problem became acute. Suddenly Chepstow, a small border town, had to cope with damage to the roads, demands for public conveniences, increased post office hours, and employ an extra lamplighter to light the lamps on the road to the new shipyard. As he was local and an authority on architecture Tipping was asked by the Admiralty to pacify the people of Chepstow who were agitated by all the work being done by military and conscript labour and the serious lack of housing for them. In April 1917 Tipping was requested to supervise a town plan, in conjunction with the Admiralty architects, to domicile the workers of the shipyard. His plan showed the importance of leaving old Chepstow alone, by providing a new main artery near the railway halt with well planned housing. The Admiralty however were forced to build standard basic A1 cottages and concrete hutments very quickly to relieve the problem, as some 30,000 men were living in tented accommodation. Endless letters of protest appeared in the *Weekly Argus* as families were squeezed into tiny houses, sleeping several to a room. Tipping had been very successful with his planning of the Homfray Road area at Rhiwbina, but when he tried to advise the Admiralty about housing in Chepstow, in the post-war retrenchment, his plans failed to get adequate support.

Although *Country Life* tried to capture the mood of Britain at the end of the war with articles on 'The re-creation of the Countryside', 'Shooting after the War', 'The revival of Cricket' and 'The future of Gundogs', the sad reality was that Britain had changed forever. It was only too obvious to Tipping when he wrote in *Country Life,*

To prevent buildings from becoming ruinous and gardens reverting to wilderness is now the utmost REALISABLE aim. Far behind us seem the easy affluent times when everyone was making, enlarging, perfecting and adorning gardens. How many of these little paradises of recent creation are doomed to future waste?

Chequers and other garden commissions

IN 1909 Sir Arthur Lee, KGB, MP and his American heiress wife Ruth, took a long lease on Chequers in Buckinghamshire. The house, nestling in the Chiltern Hills, had been gothicised in the early nineteenth century and covered with stucco. Bertram Astley had nearly completed chipping away the stucco to reveal the warm red brickwork, removing the gothic battlements and finials and replacing the windows with stone mullions when the Lees took over the tenancy. In the January 1909 edition of *Country Life* it was described as a,

> ... beautiful old house with many historic associations and restored and partially rebuilt in 1566 ... situated in the centre of the Park of about 300 acres, and ... approached by two drives with entrance lodges. It is of Tudor character, in red brick with old stone mullioned windows, and presents a pleasing and dignified appearance. The House contains a lofty central hall 33ft square, with gallery, dining room 37ft x 21ft, drawing room 37ft x 21ft, fine library 83ft x 16ft, morning room, smoking room and boudoir and there are some 30 bed and dressing rooms ... extensive stabling, and shooting over 2,700 acres including some 600 acres of covert.

The exterior lived up to their expectations, but the interior was in a bad state of repair. However, they both fell in love with the house and set about restoring it with the aid of the architect Reginald Blomfield (1856–1942). Blomfield was reputed to be excellent at restoring old houses and had already designed a terrace along the south front for the Astleys. He added an imposing porch to the entrance, reinstated the blocked off windows, and then turned his attention to the interior. Lee was adamant that it should look like a real Elizabethan house and he imported panelling, doorways and fireplaces from elsewhere. On Friday 28 January 1910 the Lees gave a dinner for 200 workmen in the nearly completed Great Hall. Ruth Lee recorded it in her diary,

LEFT Photograph by Mark Fiennes of the sunken rose garden at Chequers published in Norma Major's book on Chequers in 1996.

dinner for 200 workmen in the Great Hall at 7.30. Our first party – done by caterers at Aylesbury. Long tables decorated with plants by Smith. Mr. Blomfield at table of honour with A. and I.

And followed on Tuesday 1 February with, 'We've actually moved in to Chequers!' There was still much work to be finished, but they believed the only way to get the contractors out was to move in themselves. Ruth felt parts of the house still resembled, 'scenes from the San Francisco earthquake'. Work must have continued at a good pace, as by the end of May they were giving their house-warming party with the Roosevelts, who were attending Edward VII's funeral, Arthur Balfour, Lord Kitchener and Lord Roberts among their guests. The premature death of Delavel Astley, the heir to Chequers, in a plane crash gave the Lees the chance to buy the estate. Having finished the house, Lee turned his attention to the garden and commissioned Tipping to create an architectural setting appropriate to the newly restored house. Ruth Lee recorded that they saw Tipping's beautiful designs for the garden at Dorton House, a Jacobean mansion nearby, for Sir Lancelot and Miss Aubrey Fletcher and, 'got the idea to get his suggestions for Chequers'. Tipping was restoring Brinsop Court in Herefordshire for the Astley Family in

1911 which may have been another connection. He was a regular visitor over the next few years and signed the Chequers visitors book many times between 1910 and 1913. Ruth Lee documented his first visit,

> Sir Lancelot and Miss Aubrey Fletcher to lunch, then after Mr Tipping came and we spent a most interesting afternoon with him walking round the garden. After dinner in the Great Parlour, Mr Tipping is quite amusing and interesting and we like him very much.

The Lees must have formally engaged him in October of 1910,

> Mr. Tipping arrived about 3 and almost immediately started with Smith to lay out the new orchard. Tipping into tea and after talking about gardens. I took him round the house, showed him pictures etc. connected with the history of the house wh. he is to write for *Country Life*. After dinner showed Mr. T the Cromwell Mask and papers connected with Lady M. Grey and he showed us photos of his house.

Tipping must have then produced his plan because when he next visited in early January 1911, she wrote,

> Mr. Tipping arrived – after dinner which was quite pleasant we sat in the Long Gallery. I talked to Mr. T. Mr. Tipping's brother died only this week, but he wrote that he would come just the same as it would be "a pleasant change after the funeral."! He seems remarkably cheerful & much interested in his new estates.

The Lees were obviously unsure about his plans as the next day she tried to break it gently that they intended to do very little indeed to the garden that year and could not afford to spend much. In her diary she added, 'I did not tell him Blomfield criticised so severely the forecourt of his plan!'

In spite of Blomfield's criticism they must have decided to adopt the plan as over the next two years it was implemented as it stood. In fact the next time

LEFT Tipping's garden design for Chequers, 1910.
ABOVE The forecourt with piers taken from an example at
Canons Ashby with steeple finials.

Tipping was at Chequers he was invited as a guest at a
grand weekend house party in July in the company of the
Agnews (Lockett Agnew was the well known art dealer
and chairman of Agnews), Sibyl Colefax (society interior
decorator), the de Laszlos (Philip de Laszlo painted
several pictures of the Lees) and Mr and Mrs Leverton
Harris (avid antique collectors). Ruth Lee recorded tea in
the Grand Parlour, walking on the terrace, and waiting
for the men to come up after dinner. It turned out they
had been discussing and admiring *The Mathematicians*

which Arthur Lee had bought as a Rembrandt from the
Earl of Ashburnham's sale (it has since been reattributed
to G. van den Eeckhout). The ladies were then taken
down to see it and Ruth wrote, 'It had enormous success
as it always does!' She recalled discussions with Tipping
about the gardens and looking at the garden plans, more
visitors, walks, talking hard after dinner about politics
and art with only *The Mathematicians* lit. The house was
so full that Tipping had to be put up in the West Lodging
temporarily furnished. The Lees concluded, 'It seems to
have been a most congenial party'.

In January 1912 Tipping was at Chequers again
discussing the garden plan. The Lees impressed on him
the need to keep the garden architecture as much Jacobean
as possible and away from William III. There were more

visits for measuring and garden discussions. Tipping's big garden houses were rejected in favour of small square ones with Jacobean roofs. In July, on another of Tipping's visits, Arthur made Ruth decide on the design for the beds in the sunken garden. She wrote, 'To bed very tired and with grave misgivings as to above mentioned design!' She was still not happy with the plans as in September she recorded,

> First lot of Dutch bricks have arrived and after a look at them, I to walk with A. desperately unhappy about the garden – I see brand new pale pink walls everywhere. A. not at all worried about the colours – or says he isn't!

The next day she had an amusing talk with Arthur about what they would do if someone offered an enormous sum for the house, and she thought she would consider it, 'if the garden is a horrid failure and the walls look pale pink'. She however cheered up when Tipping built a sample bit of wall with bricks of different colours properly mixed, but still thought it would want a lot of weathering. In early October the wall was growing on the north side of the courtyard and she was relieved about the colours but distressed, 'it does not look more rough

and uneven'. By the end of October, 'the garden walls have grown incredibly since we were last here. The north garden end wall practically all done and garden house all but roof and whole of the courtyard walls. They <u>do</u> look so nice.' Tipping had altered the drive to turn into a forecourt with gate piers designed to resemble those at Canons Ashby. In the south garden there was little shelter or privacy, so Tipping raised the south boundary with a buttressed wall and garden house at each end and with the earth dug out from the wall made a broad grass walk round a sunken garden. Steps descended to the parterre, which he wrote was, 'just sufficiently sunk to be perfectly private from the road'. On the paved terrace along the south of the house Tipping added a stone doorway to the forecourt, 'taken from a charming little example at Oundle in Northamptonshire'.

BELOW The buttressed wall which was built up with a garden house at each end. This photograph and the further black and white photographs of Chequers were all taken in 1917.
RIGHT The south terrace with 'Oundle' doorway leading into the forecourt.

The south terrace was planted by Tipping with lavender, as illustrated in a watercolour of the south front in 1920. The sunken parterre had large drifts of a limited list of perennials below the walls, while the centre contained rose beds each set with a single variety of rose. As well as the two smaller garden houses on the south side, to the north of the house Tipping designed a larger square garden house opening westwards on to the long paved walk along the north façade and eastwards on to the park. In November Ruth's diary recorded, 'A. is pleased with the garden'. In 1913 Ruth recounted visitors greatly admiring the Oundle doorway and the garden houses and in February, motoring into the new courtyard for the first time, the planting of creepers on the walls and in July, the lavender on the terrace flowering and

ABOVE Watercolour of the lavender terrace at Chequers Court in 1920. Artist unknown.

RIGHT ABOVE Looking over the south garden to the parkland beyond.

RIGHT BELOW Watercolour of the gardens at Chequers Court by Ernest Arthur Rowe (1862–1922).

the beauty of the lime trees. She summarised 1913, 'The chief event has been the finishing of the garden here'. Sadly there was so little time to enjoy Tipping's design as the Great War was brewing and Chequers became a military hospital.

Tipping wrote three articles about Chequers in *Country Life* in 1917 explaining,

The character of the house seemed to demand spacious restfulness and simple dignity in its immediate environment. Hence the great unbroken north lawn and the reticent treatment of the more detailed south garden. Its paved terrace was almost exclusively planted with lavender, the grassway is of Quaker-like simplicity. Of deliberate purpose were many favourite modern features – such as pergola, dry wall, alpinery – excluded, as uncalled for by the character of the site.

LEFT The west section of the grassway seen through a garden house doorway.
ABOVE One of the smaller garden houses as it is today.

Sir Arthur and Lady Lee were obviously delighted with the articles as Ruth Lee wrote the following letter to *Country Life,*

Chequers,
October 7th, 1917.

Dear Mr. Tipping, -
We are delighted on every ground but one that you are writing the new articles on Chequers, but we should feel it a misfortune if the merits of the gardens round the house should be slurred over merely because you designed them. At the same time, we understand your reluctance to write about your own work, and only wish that the task could have been entrusted to other hands less trammelled by self-consciousness! It is

LEFT Officers convalescing on the terrace during the First World War. Chequers was used as a voluntary hospital for wounded soldiers from 1914–16.
RIGHT *The Last Days at Chequers*, Lord and Lady Lee of Fareham at the time of their leaving Chequers, New Year 1921, painting by Philip de Laszlo.

also difficult for us to criticise impartially, but everyone agrees that your treatment of a difficult and delicate problem could not have been bettered, and that you have been singularly successful, not merely in giving Chequers what it most lacked – an adequate frame for an old and beautiful picture – but in reviving, in an ingenious and happier form, the ancient setting of the house. What you recall as the "bare and staring" walls have long since become mellowed and clothed, and the brick skeleton of your "lay-out" has blended with its surroundings in a way which is as charming to the eye as it is convenient for its purpose. There is much more that we could say, but, in spite of war-time neglect, the pictures speak for themselves!

Yours sincerely,

RUTH LEE.

Tipping added that, 'much of the merits of the scheme were largely due to the apt suggestions and criticisms which Sir Arthur and Lady Lee made during the course of the work'. In 1917 after lengthy discussions with the then Prime Minister, David Lloyd George, the childless Lees decided to bequeath Chequers to the nation as a country retreat for the serving Prime Minister. Whereas before the war, Prime Ministers had always belonged to the landed gentry, the post-war era was bringing in a new breed of politician without country houses to entertain foreign dignitaries, or a tranquil place to relax from the affairs of state. Lord and Lady Lee of Fareham, as they then became, finally left Chequers on 8 January 1921. The stained glass window in the long gallery bears the following inscription,

This house and peace and ancient memories was given to England as a thank-offering for her deliverance in the great war of 1914–1918 as a place of rest and recreation for her Prime Ministers for ever.

A portrait of the Lees, *The Last Days at Chequers*, painted by Philip de Laszlo, hangs at Chequers to mark their departure in 1921.

The house and gardens at Chequers have remained virtually unchanged for more than eighty years. Heads of State and Prime Ministers have added memorial trees in the parkland, a continued tradition since David Lloyd George planted the first of them in 1917 as the first Prime Minister to occupy Chequers. Apart from an orangery added recently on one side of the sunken area, Tipping's garden is still intact.

Brinsop Court, Herefordshire

Brinsop Court, built about 1350, is a moated manor house. It was frequently visited by the poet William Wordsworth after his wife's brother had rented the property in the 1820s. Wordsworth planted the cedar tree at Brinsop in 1827 but this was felled by a storm when Tipping was staying at the house in 1917. By 1909, when Tipping wrote in *Country Life* that although Brinsop stood, 'so entirely enjoyable, so free from discordant notes, so completely picturesque', it had fallen into a neglected state and needed 'reparation

BELOW Brinsop Court with the Wordsworth cedar planted by the poet in 1827. This and the black and white photographs of Brinsop on the following pages were published in the *Country Life* articles of 1908 and 1914.

RIGHT Watercolour of northwest angle of the courtyard by Gwen Dorrien-Smith in 1921.

OVERLEAF The courtyard garden looking west with flower beds, a stone vase in the centre, trees in tubs recently planted in 1914.

of a careful, knowledgeable and restrained kind'. This neglected opportunity must have appealed to Mr and Mrs Hubert Astley, since they bought the property in 1911 and Tipping then advised on the laying out of the gardens and restoration of the house with the approval of William Weir and the Society for the Protection of Ancient Buildings. It was a major restoration with an entirely new wing on the eastern end of the courtyard. Inside Tipping was responsible for restoring most of the principal rooms. Tipping accurately replaced the screen in the oak parlour. The Elizabethan solar became the library with overmantel and wainscoting taken from Mildmay House in Clerkenwell and is similar to the oak parlour at Mounton, built at the same time. Tipping added his name in Latin on the bench ends in the Banqueting Hall. These rooms survive almost completely unchanged since their restoration by Tipping.

Tipping also laid out the courtyard garden with borders and statues making it, 'a charming little domain of peace'. On the south side a low dry-stone wall was made above the lawn with circular steps from the terrace

LEFT The names of Henry Tipping and the Keeble brothers carved in Latin on a bench end in the Banqueting Hall in commemoration of their restoration work at Brinsop Court.
RIGHT ABOVE The Elizabethan solar at Brinsop, now furnished and fitted as the library of Lady Sutton (Hubert Astley's wife) with ceiling copied from Broughton Castle in Oxfordshire.
RIGHT BELOW The screen in the oak parlour believed to be inspired by one made by Robert Lorimer for Earlshall in Fife.

and a long herbaceous border above. Hubert Astley was a well-known ornithologist with a large collection of exotic birds. Tipping divided the moat with a bridge and added a pergola to make an area for his flamingos, as shown in the watercolour by Gwen Dorrien-Smith painted in 1921. The bones of Tipping's garden can still be seen, but the pergola and some of the planting have now disappeared.

LEFT ABOVE Steps from the terrace lead to the lawn at Brinsop Court.

LEFT BELOW Watercolour of the south side with dry-stone wall planted with drifts of herbaceous plants by Gwen Dorrien-Smith, 1921.

BELOW Tipping divided the moat with a bridge and added a pergola to make an area for Hubert Astley's flamingos seen in this watercolour by Gwen Dorrien-Smith.

Yews, Windermere, Cumbria

Tipping was asked to advise on the gardens at Yews by Lady Anne Scott, mother of the present owner, Sir Oliver Scott, although the diary of 1908 suggests he may have already advised on the additions to the house. His design for the sunken garden with Irish yews dated 1912 is the only original garden plan by Tipping to have been found. Thomas Mawson (1861–1933) had already worked on the garden in 1902, when he was working at Blackwell also on the Storrs estate for Sir Edward Holt. Tipping worked with Lady Scott, who was a keen gardener, on the formal gardens near to the house, with yew hedging, topiary, rose garden and croquet lawn. The oak summerhouse with sliding doors was probably added by Tipping. There is also a Messenger glasshouse with beaver-tail glass which is exactly the same model as Tipping's own glasshouse at High Glanau. A copy of Tipping's thank-you letter written in 1912 still survives,

Mathern Palace, Chepstow.
July 22nd., 1912.

My dear Annie,

Your Lancashire roads were quite horrid and the scenery of the industrial districts woefully depressing. But I got to Wardley Hall all right and thence went on to Altringham and lunched there. Thence onwards to my journeys end the scene changed and I passed through delightful Cheshire and Shropshire country reaching Adcote [where Tipping advised the Darby family on the garden] at six o'clock for a cup of tea and a great deal of garden talk before dinner. I stayed there till after lunch yesterday and came on here in four hours and a quarter. It is fully a hundred miles so I am afraid we exceeded the speed limit; but the roads were excellent and there was not much traffic.

Here I find much sunshine and there has been no heavy rain during the ten days I was away except on Saturday. Evidently we are very droughty compared with your lake-land so you may expect me to come falling in upon you to get damp at unexpected moments.

I greatly enjoyed my visit to you. That motor round to the Tarns and to Coniston water was absolutely delightful.

I was very glad to see too how very satisfactorily the "Georgian saloons" coalesce with the "Westmoreland homestead." I was afraid the two blocks of building might jar, but the whole thing really groups together picturesquely, and one does not feel any jar at the strongly marked change of style.

I am going to be exceedingly busy for two or three days and then will explain my notes, etc. as to the garden to my assistant so that you may have a plan of what was decided on as soon as possible.

Sincerely yours
H.Avray Tipping

OPPOSITE ABOVE Tipping's original garden plan for Yews, Windermere, dated 1912.
OPPOSITE BELOW LEFT The sunken garden with Irish yews today.
OPPOSITE BELOW RIGHT The croquet lawn with pavilion with sliding doors designed by Tipping.

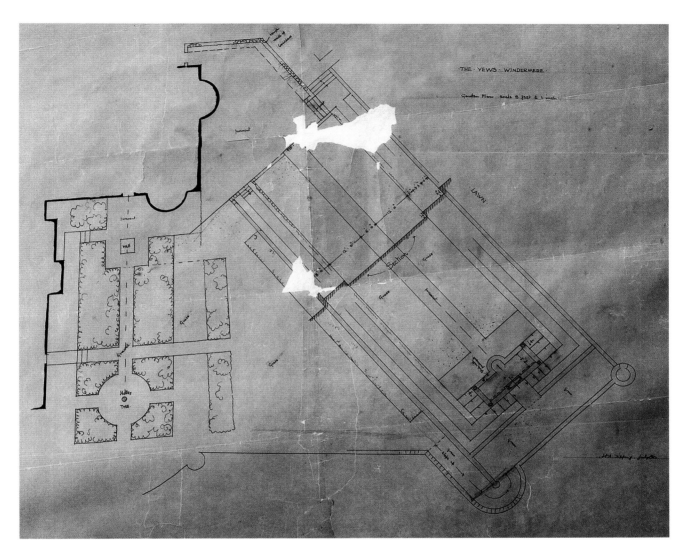

THE·YEWS·WINDERMERE·

Garden Plan Scale 8 feet to 1 inch.

149

Wyndcliffe Court, Monmouthshire

In 1922 Charles Leigh Clay, who established the Claymore Shipping Line in Cardiff, built a large Arts and Crafts stone house on a high bluff on the west side of the Wye Valley. The architect of Wyndcliffe Court was Eric Francis who, having built Mounton House in 1912, was much influenced by Tipping. Tipping was commissioned to design the garden in 1922 for the house standing on high ground facing south with views over the Bristol Channel.

Tipping designed the garden, with his customary paved terrace extended by a pair of flights of shallow steps descending to a round pool half inset beneath a scalloped hood. The pool was similar in style to the one that Lutyens incorporated in the garden at Hestercombe in 1904. He added the lawns, bowling green and summerhouse to link the different levels. The topiary was the most prominent feature of the garden; yew was planted in formal groups of complex shapes and sculptural hedges around the lawns. Tipping wrote in *The Garden of To-day*,

Topiary work is rather like drink. Against it there are ardent prohibitionists such as William Robinson, and there have been, at times, outbursts of intoxicated license. But there are also reasonable and perfectly legitimate middle courses – the moderate indulgence in well-formed hedges as well as in well-flavoured wine. I wish to be neither dry nor drunk; neither lacking in all formal tree treatment, nor surrounded by motley and fantastic yew shapes.

The bowling green on the next level is dominated by a huge pair of yew spirals. Tim Richardson writing about Wyndcliffe in the *Telegraph* in 2006 noted, 'In many Arts and Crafts gardens, topiary was used architecturally to create a sense of enclosure or mystery, but here it takes on a delightfully domestic character: the hedges are more like furniture than walls, which is unusual for a garden of this time'.

LEFT Wyndcliffe Court built by E.C. Francis for the Clay family in 1922 with garden designed by Tipping.
ABOVE Watercolour of the terrace at Wyndcliffe with view to the Severn estuary beyond by Lilian Mabel Bott (1871–1953).
RIGHT The scallop-hooded pool below the terrace. This pool is similar in style to Lutyens's pool at Hestercombe.

At the western end of the terrace, on a diagonal, is the stone summerhouse open on the far side to overlook the Severn estuary and the walled kitchen garden. The building is a two-storey construction, with the ground floor in the corner of the former orchard. This has no windows and was originally used for mushroom cultivation. The upper part with original seating overlooks the sunken garden. The steeply pitched roof is similar to the pavilions at Hidcote. The sunken garden with the small rectangular pool in the centre and the shallow terraces filled with massed bergenia, a favourite Jekyll plant, is linked to the herbaceous border above by small flights of steps with low flanking piers. Tim Richardson described the sunken garden as 'a masterpiece of subtle design, successfully hinting at a sense of enclosure, without resort to masses of stonework'. The double herbaceous borders above the sunken garden link the house with the ornamental wrought-iron gates to the kitchen garden. They are filled with oriental poppies and *Alchemilla mollis* in typical Edwardian style in wide borders. The walled kitchen garden with old glasshouses has a central gravel path and a mixture of espaliered apples and pears, raspberries and flowers for the house. Roses and wisteria cascade over the walls.

The son of Charles Leigh Clay has recently died and the house will pass to the next generation. The fact that it has remained in one family since inception means the gardens have largely remained unaltered since Tipping created them. As David Wheeler wrote in *Country Life* in 1998, 'Wyndcliffe remains secure in a romantic time warp, swathed in rose and old-world fragrance, the essence of the life of a country garden'.

ABOVE Aerial view of the gardens at Wyndcliffe.
1 Walled kitchen garden
2 Shrubbery
3 Summerhouse
4 Herbaceous borders
5 Sunken garden
6 Bowling green
7 Topiary terrace
8 Terrace with scallop-headed pool
RIGHT Yew topiary above the bowling green.

LEFT The sunken garden with bergenia massed around the pool and the house behind.
ABOVE LEFT The stone summerhouse with steeply pitched roof set on a diagonal in the sunken garden.
ABOVE RIGHT The double herbaceous borders which link the house to the kitchen garden.

Dartington Hall, Devon

In 1925 Leonard and Dorothy Elmhirst bought the Dartington Hall estate to create a utopian experiment in rural reconstruction and a famously progressive school. William Weir was in charge of the restoration of the buildings. Tipping and Weir had worked together at Brinsop Court. The design of the garden was coordinated by Dorothy, in consultation with Tipping in 1928, then with Beatrix Farrand in 1933 after Tipping's death and after 1945 with Percy Cane. Dorothy had recognised that the garden landscape had great possibilities, with its natural contours, magnificent trees and its historical and architectural features, but after clearing the brambles and overgrown ivy, she realised that she needed outside

gardening expertise. Tipping was then in his early seventies, but with his versatility, knowledge of architecture, success in journalism and experience in horticulture and garden design, the Elmhirsts felt,

> altogether he seemed a fairly safe choice for Dartington: he had been an eager disciple of William Robinson and Gertrude Jekyll in their campaign for 'natural planting' and was clearly no extremist. He was known to believe in a mixture of the calculated and the unconstrained, and his normal practice was to compose a formal design in immediate relation to a house, which then merged into the naturalism of woodland – and where possible, water – further off.

The Elmhirsts wanted to learn from Tipping whether it might be possible to develop the garden, both as an amenity and at the same time, as a commercial venture – one obvious implication of the 'Dartington experiment'. They exchanged letters with Tipping over an extended period during which it appeared that Tipping was playing 'hard to get' as he kept postponing the visit. Leonard Elmhirst particularly, 'wanted him to see the garden in winter, in relation to the future planning of the garden, the courtyard, the drive and other features'. Eventually Tipping agreed in February 1927, 'to visit to think out a scheme and take all necessary measurements, levels and notes'. He suggested working in harness with William Weir who was in charge of the medieval fabric at Dartington. On 16 February 1927 Tipping wrote to Mrs Elmhirst,

> My recollection of the Sunday at Dartington is that of an earthly paradise. Mr. Weir coming to lunch here on Friday. Meanwhile I shall be able to give most of to-day

LEFT Dorothy and Leonard Elmhirst in 1925.
RIGHT Dartington Hall, c.1927.

are essential if one is to take the right kind of interest in garden reconstruction....I have insisted from the start that the bread and butter end of this experiment must come first, and that we are not an ordinary country house for entertainment. We have therefore sacrificed the ornamental garden this time for the production end. This does not mean that I do not value the former, but that the following out of Mr. Tipping's plan cannot always be carried through immediately.

In fact, both Weir and Tipping did visit in September 1927 for a shared working weekend and were jointly responsible for the loggia near the front door of the private house. Tipping's notes, still in the Dartington archives, dated 22 September, for the garden outside the entrance archway include, 'enclosing wall – steps through middle of wall opening' and for the private garden, 'terrace 30 feet – yew at end, 10 foot border'. Tipping submitted his final plan in 1928 for the private area between the house and the tiltyard, the medieval jousting ground. He designed yew hedging at the end of the bowling green to separate it from the Great Lawn. He used the sunken ruined arches of the arcade as an architectural feature in the garden layout. He had already designed something similar at his old home Mathern Palace with the ruined bishop's palace. At Dartington the arches were probably the window heads of a long gallery that gave spectators a clear view of the tiltyard below. Tipping built a retaining wall on either side of the arches, and a low stone wall the full length of the bowling green above the twelve apostle yews and tiltyard and established the long herbaceous border which became known as 'Dorothy's Sunny Border'.

Tipping also recommended Stewart Lynch as the first garden superintendent, found through the director of Kew Gardens. Lynch had been trained by his father, Richard Lynch, curator of the Cambridge University Botanic Garden and, after appointments at Lyon and Versailles, he worked for the Rothschild family near Cannes, followed by two years service with the Imperial War Graves Commission. Lynch worked at Dartington from 1928 until his retirement in 1943. Tipping wrote to Elmhirst in November 1928, 'I have seen Lynch, we had a

or tomorrow to jotting down a sort of rough plan of the suggestion which I made to you and which we agreed upon, both for the great court and the terrace gardens.

Tipping wrote in August to ask if his plans for autumn and winter work were being carried out but Leonard Elmhirst obviously felt there was too much happening and sent Weir a letter dated 12 August 1927,

Mr. Tipping has suggested coming again – could you connect up with him and pay us a visit about the same time? I am afraid he may be very disappointed at our not having done anything this summer to the garden, but it is quite impossible to do everything at once; and, as you know, with a gang of 200 men on construction work of one kind or another, with a school into the bargain, it has not been easy to find the time and the leisure which long talk on Dartington, and I feel certain that the garden there is safe in his hands'. One of Lynch's first tasks was to complete the Sunny Border and make the stone path beside it, renovate the bowling green and plant the yew hedges advocated by Tipping. By August 1929 Tipping considered his professional connection with the work at Dartington closed and sent a bill for a hundred guineas.

BELOW Dartington Hall seen through the twelve apostle yews. The photograph shows the restored medieval hall in 1965.
RIGHT ABOVE The ruined arches of the banqueting house above the tiltyard at Dartington Hall which Tipping incorporated into his garden plan dated 1927.
RIGHT BELOW 'Dorothy's Sunny Border' below the bowling green today.

Other garden commissions

Besides designing his own gardens and the ones already described, Tipping also advised other friends. At Buckland Hall at Talybont on Usk in Powys he advised Mrs Gwynne-Holford on some of the formal gardens there (left above). His friend Morgan Stuart Williams of St Donat's Castle designed the central sundial and Tipping himself designed a lily garden on the steep hillside running down to the river Usk (left below). On the death of her husband, Mrs Gwynne-Holford moved to Hartpury in Gloucestershire. Tipping suggested a planting of rhododendrons and azaleas at Hartpury, where the gardens had been designed by Thomas Mawson for the Gordon-Canning family in 1907. The Buckland estate was bought by Lord Buckland, an industrialist and newspaper magnate who commissioned Tipping to design a tennis pavilion in 1926 (top right). The octagonal pavilion is delightfully executed, still with its original interior with stone fireplace, kitchen with wooden sink and outside a veranda and blinds. Sadly the enchanting formal gardens at Buckland no longer exist. All that remains are a few large Irish yews, some golden yew hedging, steps up to the woodland and an abandoned walled garden and glasshouses.

Tipping designed a garden pavilion at Benham Valance in Berkshire (below right) in 1915 for Sir Richard Vincent Sutton, the stepson of Hubert Astley of Brinsop Court. At Clytha Park in Monmouthshire he added an Irish yew avenue to link the house to the D plan walled kitchen garden in the 1920s, and a double avenue of apple trees by the canalised stream leading to the lake. Also in the 1920s he was asked by the Aldrich-Blake family to add a new wing to the Elizabethan house at Weston Hall in Herefordshire and he designed a large tennis pavilion there (centre right) as well as a dog kennel. In the late 1920s he advised Gwendoline and Margaret Davies on the woodland and dell garden at Gregynog in Powys. Tipping is also known to have designed the garden at Old Buckenham Hall in Norfolk, as well as a rose garden and colonnades at Wootton House, Butleigh Wootton in Somerset.

High Glanau, Monmouthshire

I N 1922 Tipping embarked on his *pièce de résistance*, his last country house and garden. Tipping had bought the Trellech estate of 1,640 acres, initially for rough shooting for his friends in 1917. He sold off some of the land, cottages and farmhouses in a sale by auction by John D. Wood & Co. on 10 September 1917.

The land was situated on high ground above Monmouth, on the west of the ridge dividing the rivers Usk and Wye. The gradient was steep, but there had been a crofter's primitive dwelling with arable land around it which formed a flat area above the woodland and it was here that Tipping decided to build his last Monmouthshire home, High Glanau. Tipping described it,

ABOVE Watercolour by G.H. Kitchin of Lloysey Farm on the Trellech estate which Tipping bought in 1917.
RIGHT Pencil sketch of High Glanau in 1926 by G.H. Kitchin.

High Planau
Monmouth. July 2 26

Just where the bit of arable met the scrub, where the fairly level and fully open was cheek by jowl with the tree-dotted and rugged woodland, space was found for the proposed dwelling and for a sufficient approach without unduly wounding nature's curves with geometrical cuts and harsh embankments.

The house itself is delightfully unpretentious, his simplest home, nestling in a clearing amid rock-strewn woodland and on a natural plateau. Tipping believed, 'a house should sit at ease with nature and so it should have no harsh angles or intrusive features' and, unlike many of his contemporaries, he rejoiced in the idea of various levels in a garden.

Tipping used the warm-coloured sandstone of the county which occurs both in block and in laminating strata, so it was equally suitable for the house and for the garden walls and paving. The same texture and tone therefore unifies both house and garden in a traditional Arts and Crafts style. The house faced west, high and stark, so Tipping chose a thick Pembrokeshire slate for the roofs and for hanging the upper storey, as weather-tightness was a primary object. He described the tile as having a silver green sheen, but

BELOW Photograph of garden façade at High Glanau, taken for Tipping's article in 1929.
RIGHT Garden façade of High Glanau as it is today.

as fairly thick and rough of edge and surface, but not over heavy and sufficiently smooth to lie flat. He further explained, 'Eaves were reduced to a minimum, the idea being not merely that the structure should withstand the climatic assaults, but should show its meaning clearly on its face'.

Again this was in collaboration with the young Chepstow architect Eric Francis, but this time Tipping wanted a much smaller, almost cottage-style retreat with generously proportioned accommodation finished to a particularly high standard, where he could write his books and hone his gardening ideas. On the entrance front, a broad slated roof sweeps down, punctuated by two gabled turrets, one slate-hung for the porch and the other of random stones for the stairs.

Roderick Gradidge, author of *Dream Houses – The Edwardian Ideal*, described it as, 'beautifully handled: the roof sweeps down low, broken by two short gabled wings, and the front door is treated completely unpretentiously'. On the west garden façade there are three slate-hung gables, framed by a pair of chimneys. Tipping explained, somewhat dismissively, 'The house has no architectural pretensions or special style. Ample sweeps of roof and a few gables satisfy utility and agree with the landscape.' But Penny Churchill, writing in the property page in *Country Life* in 2002 considered that, 'Modern experts might beg to differ, for High Glanau, now listed Grade II, is surely an excellent example of Arts and Crafts architecture at its most appealing, with its warm sandstone walls, leaded casements, stone window frames and mullions and liberal

interior use of ashlar and oak'. The stone window frames and mullions of a similar warm pink hue were cut from the Hollington quarries in Staffordshire, as the local stone was too hard and too peppered with quartz pebbles to be used as ashlar. Wood window framing was used for the lighter structures. The leaded casements were consistent with the interior liberal use of oak, an ideal of the first quarter of the seventeenth century which Tipping cherished and used in all his homes. The whole layout of the house is asymmetrical. A projection on the kitchen end gave protection to the north end of the upper terrace. A garage and yard were twisted into a semi-level spot on the north and near it, a three-roomed bungalow for guests. Tipping stated, 'there is nothing odd or straggly about the appearance of the group, because it is clearly a

practical and sympathetic fitting of a little human effort into great natural features'. Inside he wanted, 'a cottage plan with considerable amplitude'. His own sketch plan shows the interior layout of the house.

The cottage plan was made by, 'the disposition of the central living-room, twenty-four feet square and lit on both sides with a parlour at one end and kitchens on the other'. Tipping found an oak beam 25 feet in length and 18 inches in depth in the Monmouth timber merchant's yard to span the width of the central room ceiling. Smaller beams stretched out from it to form six plasterwork panels taken, 'from an Early Elizabethan example'. Tipping decided to continue the use of the Hollington stone for the chimneypiece and walls in the living room. The room was lit from both sides and he

LEFT The entrance side of High Glanau in 1929.

RIGHT Tipping's sketch plan of High Glanau house and terraces, 1929.

1 Entrance 2 Living room
3 Parlour 4 Den 5 Loggia
6 Lobby 7 Kitchen
8 Back lobby 9 Larders
10 Lobby 11 Bedroom
12 Woodshed 13 Garage yard
14 Entrance side
15 Sycamore trees 16 Pool
17 South terrace
18 Upper west terrace
19 Lower west terrace
20 Dry wall and path
21 Octagonal pool 22 Oak
and hazels 23 Steps down
through rocks 24 Grass level
25 Path between borders
26 Hedge of *Lonicera nitida*
27 Broad grassway between
borders 28 Treillage above
dry wall

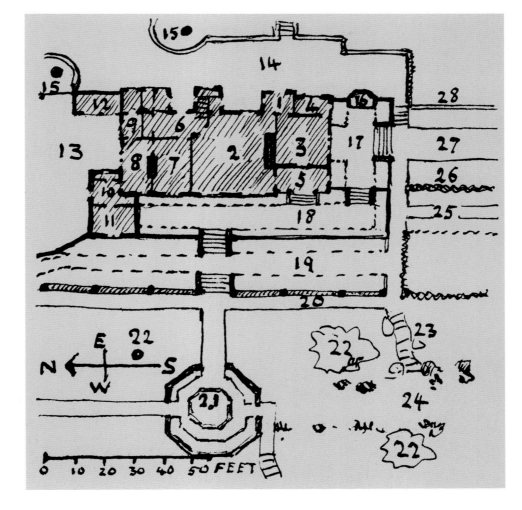

used random oak boards for the floor. This central room was similar to the oak room that he created for himself at Mathern Palace. His considerable collection of old oak furniture, carvings, pewter and porcelain moved from house to house with him. Some pieces are illustrated in Percy Macquoid's *Dictionary of English Furniture* published in 1924–27. The sweep of the main roof allowed a garden room with sliding doors overlooking the terrace, where Tipping could take his meals in the fresh air, and a small workroom on the parlour side. The parlour, where

Tipping wrote his books and articles for *Country Life*, was panelled in oak, 'drawn out foot by foot to suit the various pictures and ornaments that are set on it and the bookcases that are sunk within it'. Again there was a fine plasterwork ceiling.

By building the house and garden together, Tipping could line up all the windows with the garden features; the oak room window looked down the steps to the octagonal pool and his study window aligned with the herbaceous border and pergola.

BELOW The central living room with table set for one in 1929.

RIGHT ABOVE The Hollington stone chimneypiece.

RIGHT BELOW Tipping's parlour with panelling made to fit his furniture and pictures.

Once Tipping had settled the site and plan of the house, he turned his attention to the immediate garden around it. He did not agree with John Rea's seventeenth-century view that, 'the most graceful ground is an entire level' but thought, 'where the lie of the land is much broken, a flat stretch or two certainly add to the setting of a house, and are agreeable to both eye and movement'. So he made a level site the width of the house on the south side, separating it from the slope above by a three foot dry-stone wall. A grassway ran down the centre and on either side were two herbaceous borders, 100 feet in length, planted in hues of yellow and blue with achilleas, heleniums, delphiniums, irises, michaelmas daisies and violas. Tipping called this the ribbon parterre. There was a gravel path on one side and a *Lonicera nitida* hedge on

the other, giving a sense of enclosure. In *Historic Gardens of England* Lady Rockley wrote that Tipping was one of the first to discover the properties of *Lonicera nitida* as a hedging shrub and that its use at High Glanau was impressive. This was one of the earliest uses of this plant for formal hedging in Britain.

To the south Tipping built a high stone wall, shaped to allow for the gradient. Behind this was an open and sunny spot which he made into his frameyard and working area with a glasshouse. The glasshouse, built in 1923 by Messenger & Co. some 40 feet long, still exists, with beaver-tail glass to keep rainwater off the wood, original hot water pipes, cast-iron window ratchets and the grape vine planted by Tipping. A large potting shed with wooden bench was set into the frameyard side of

LEFT The ribbon parterre
looking towards the house
in 1929.
RIGHT The restored
Messenger & Co.
greenhouse built in 1923.
BELOW The ribbon parterre
looking towards the pergola
in 1929.

LEFT The ribbon parterre looking towards the pergola today.

RIGHT Commemorative wall plaque installed within the pergola when it was restored.

BELOW The pergola, restored in 2005.

Here lived
H·AVRAY TIPPING
who made this garden
in 1923

the wall, near at hand for the gardeners. At the south end of the ribbon parterre, a pergola the width of the parterre and with four massive cylindrical columns was set against the other side of the wall. The pillars of the pergola are still the original stone columns, but the oak beams have been recently restored with a grant from CADW (the Welsh equivalent of English Heritage) to copy those in the old photographs.

From the house the grassway between the herbaceous borders was reached by steps from a flagged and bedded plat that lay in front of the south side. The east end was sheltered by another high stone wall, recessed in the middle to contain a stone tank. Here water fell into an old stone trough and then descended into a basin below, so that the constant running of water added movement to

the garden. The water to the tank was pumped up by a Blake's hydraulic ram set in the stream 200 feet below the house. It threw up 8,000 gallons every twenty-four hours into a reservoir in the garden of the gardener's cottage which was above the house roof level; so there was, and still is, water all day long falling from the trough into the basin and then by underground pipe, to the fountain on the octagonal pool. Originally the water was used again for rills either side of the pool filled with colonies of iris, primula and astilbe.

The *Lonicera nitida* hedge, on the lower side of the ribbon parterre, stood on a low dry-stone wall and borders of lupins in June, followed by *Sedum spectabile* and *Aster thomsonii* and amellus, lined the central gravel path below it. Pear trees were trained along a framework

LEFT Tipping's wisteria
and *Clematis montana* var.
rubens climb around the
parlour window.
ABOVE The tank on the
four bedded plat in 1929.
RIGHT The tank as it is now.
FAR RIGHT The Blake's
hydraulic ram on the
stream bed.

to give the path a feeling of seclusion. Behind this were vegetables and flowers for cutting, which struck, 'a utilitarian cottage note'. This area now has lawn with a lavender lined path, as the tree growth has made the slope too dark for growing vegetables, which are now grown in the frameyard.

On the west side of the house the rapid fall of the hillside needed different treatment. Stepping out from the garden loggia, the full glory of the site was revealed. From the terraces and beyond the octagonal pool, the land became increasingly rugged, falling away into a valley wooded with deciduous trees, a stream and ancient grist mill. It was the perfect blend of formal and natural which Tipping recommended at the Royal Horticultural Society conference in 1928, 'Let there be some formalism about the house to carry on the geometric lines and enclosed feeling of architecture, but let us step shortly from that into wood and wild garden'.

Now, as then, the land rises again from the dell, this time more gradually and the eye is drawn up over a patchwork of green fields, skimming over the picturesquely sited Cwmcarvan church until at a glance it encompasses the sweep of west Monmouthshire and its meeting with the Brecon Beacons on the horizon. To the right comes the gap in the hills, where the town of Abergavenny nestles between the Blorenge and the Sugar Loaf mountains, against the backdrop of the Black Mountains. Tipping understood the challenge thrown down by such a view, and he embraced it by splashing massed colours of irises, peonies, erigerons and crocosmias right at your feet on the upper terrace borders, drawing the focus back in. The limit to this formal area of the garden is the dry-stone wall which

supports the lower terrace. Eight masonried piers add support but also give the wall an architectural quality which links it back to the house above. Tipping topped these piers with huge hand hewn sandstone balls.

The dry wall serves to contain the formal garden, but Tipping wrote, 'The lie of the land happily suggested a dovetailing instead of a rigid boundary between the wild and the formal'. The lower west terrace, that lay between the retaining wall of the upper terrace and the dry-stone wall, had borders wide enough to hold delicate shrubs such as cistuses, veronicas, fuchsias and hypericums and on the other side of the paved way, a greater profusion of peonies, erigerons and irises.

Sadly the sandstone balls have been stolen, but there are plans for their replacement with a grant from CADW. Just below the terraces, Tipping realised there was a little area of cuplike appearance which, with a bit of embanking and spade work, was the ideal site for a lily pond, octagonal with a paved surround and partly enclosing wall. Tipping

LEFT ABOVE Sedum path running to the frameyard, with pear trees trained on the trellis in 1929.

LEFT BELOW The lavender walk as it is today.

RIGHT View from the terrace down the steps to the octagonal pool.

OVERLEAF View towards the Sugar Loaf and Skirrid from the west terrace.

planted penstemon in the borders, but today this is the soft bluey-mauve of lavender through which pink roses rise, delicate against the warm stone.

Tipping wrote, 'there is nothing really wild at Glanau. There are woodlands more or less treated, more or less left to native vegetation, more or less swept and garnished. It is gardening, but with nature kept in the forefront of set purpose.' Tipping made a plan of the upper and lower woodland gardens. From the rough stone steps below the corner of the house and terraces, the upper garden followed a northwards path through an area of gardened wood. Tipping planted eucryphias, viburnums, magnolias, forsythias, deutzias, hydrangeas and *Rhododendron* 'Pink Pearl', newly introduced to Britain. At first the rhododendrons lacked sustenance in the soil and grew leggy and flowerless, but Tipping gave, 'a generous dressing of poultry manure which effected a rapid transformation. Leaves became a wholesome green and flower buds formed profusely. They have been a success ever since.' Eighty years later, the *Rhododendron* 'Pink Pearl' and other rhododendrons and azaleas that he planted still make a great show for the garden open day for the National Gardens Scheme. There

LEFT ABOVE The upper west terrace in May.
LEFT BELOW The lower west terrace in June.
BELOW The dry-stone wall with its sentinel piers in 1929.
OVERLEAF The octagonal pool with box balls today.

is now a natural pond below the terraces, probably made from a damp area under the original iris rills.

Along the paths in the upper wood Tipping planted phlox and hydrangeas. The variety of *Hydrangea* 'Souvenir de Mme Chautre', with splendid metallic blue heads, was, 'a special feature and planted by the score'. Tipping originally had statues of Bacchus and Mercury as focal points in these woods. Sadly these are no longer there but the plinths remain as a reminder of the lost garden. The mossy pathways that criss-cross this woodland area, through the heathers and rhododendrons, still provide a delightful place for a pensive walk with their sudden vistas to the valley below and visual surprises such as the yew tree growing out of the boulder. Tipping noted, 'The making of the path by its side meant a little lowering of the level and gave enhanced presence to the yew'.

A winding, many stepped path descends into the lower woodland giving glimpses of the stream below, from which can be heard the murmur of water. Here we find Tipping in his most Robinsonian mode. In the deep-set wood around the stream, Tipping cleared trees and undergrowth to let in sun and air and planted *Primula pulverulenta*, which he described, 'They look particularly well, running up the banks, following the course of the little springs to their source, so that its tall, many-tiered candelabra rise out of their bunches of big leaves above the eye line'. He went on to write about the varieties of primula, also flourishing wherever he set them,

'Bartley' 'Raby' and 'Lissadel' strains. *Primula japonica* presents itself in various hues, but the dark crimson 'Etna' is the most favoured. *Primula beesiana* and *bulleyana* and their hybrids are especially valuable as carrying on the primula season through June.

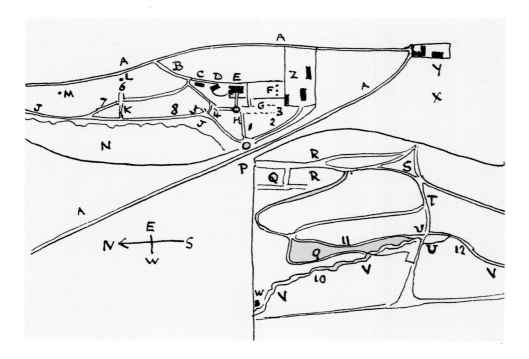

LEFT Tipping's sketch plan of the upper and lower gardens at High Glanau as published in *Country Life*, 15 June 1929. The numbers refer to illustrations in the article. Number 11 is here reproduced on page 187.
A Private road   B Drive
C Bungalow   D Garage
E House   F Pergola
G Natural terrace
H Pathway to lower garden
J Path through wood
K Cross path looking up to statue   L.M Statues
N Open bank
O Gate out of upper garden
P Gate into lower garden
Q Rectangular grassways
R Birch thicket
S Sunny bank
T Path down to old mill race
U Little ram and mill race
V Line of the stream
W Large ram   X Meadow
Y Farmery and cottages
Z Greenhouses, potting sheds etc.
RIGHT The rustic steps which lead from the lower woodland walks back to the house.

As ever, there was a small pool set above a waterfall for bathing during hot summer days.

Tipping dedicated a special area to ferns, which were self-set but assisted to full development by clearing the weeds. He explained,

> Here the fall is rapid and the streamlet in dancing mood as it cascades down or whirls round rocks. It is a delightful spot in dry summer weather. Even in the drought of 1921, the ground was damp in the dell, and the ferns brilliantly green.

Tipping admitted in a letter to William Robinson that he and his gardeners always kept *The English Flower Garden* handy for constant reference and in *English Gardens*, he acknowledged his debt to Robinson, 'although I have ever remained a formalist when formalism appears to me apt and fitting, yet it is largely through him that I have added to this the wide and joyous domains of wood and wild'.

The garden at High Glanau was Tipping's swansong. After the war with its profound loss of so many jobbing gardeners, he wanted a house and garden on a reduced scale. It was here that he was able to indulge the passionate and informed gardening interests that he shared with Jekyll and Robinson. He wrote,

> Nor have we come to the end – or nearly to the end – of new forms, new combinations, new plants. The movement towards extensive, rather than intensive, gardening largely occasioned by high wages and

BELOW The upper woodland as it is now.
RIGHT Stone path and steps in the lower woodland in Tipping's time.

straitened purses, is almost in its infancy. The right and spacious setting of the infinite number of beautiful trees and flowering shrubs on broken grounds and woodland wastes is a development which rightly excites and occupies the garden lover today.

High Glanau was Tipping's favourite home and garden. Unlike Mathern Palace and Mounton, which were substantial and imposing houses and gardens, High Glanau is perhaps his most personal. Here, out of all his gardens, his design shows complete harmony between house and garden, which he then continued into the landscape beyond. The compact scale of the formal garden, the naturalistic drifts of flowers, the tranquil setting, the romantic woodland garden and the dramatic view are testament to Tipping's skill as gardener and garden designer.

When Tipping died in 1933 his Monmouthshire home was put on the market. The High Glanau estate consisting of 598 acres was sold to Colonel F.A. Hamilton, a local JP. He continued to allow the townspeople of Monmouth access to the gardens twice a year to see the herbaceous borders and the wild garden where he once noted, 'the pink spireas are at their best'. He also provided access to Atkins Hill nearby from which a glorious view of the countryside may be seen. His tenure was short as in the late 1930s Sir Beckwith Whitehouse, gynaecologist to the royal family, bought the house. Lady Whitehouse loved the garden at High Glanau. Tipping's exuberant borders lost none of their charm and the garden was filled with Sir Beckwith's students and with family and friends sitting on the terraces and picking strawberries, and small boys paddling in the octagonal pool. The royal family sent the heathers, planted in oval beds showing splashes of pinks each autumn above the top lawn. After Sir Beckwith's death in 1943, Lady Whitehouse stayed on until 1953, bequeathing part of the woodland to the Forestry Commission in memory of her son, Hugh, who loved the woods and streams. He was tragically killed in the Second World War. David Whitehouse, her grandson, clearly remembers his grandmother telling him stories of the garden, how his mother won his grandfather round by spending a wet weekend planting 2,000 tulip bulbs with him. Showing him where she was peppered in

LEFT The lower woodland – spring above the pool.
RIGHT The lower woodland today.

the leg by one of his grandfather's students on a shoot, and had hobbled back to the house alone and bleeding while the men continued after the pheasant. She remembered her son Hugh climbing on Tipping's statue of Bacchus. He remembers walking, hand in hand with his grandmother, 'following the paths down to the water garden and deeply inhaling the scent of honeysuckle and roses'. The garden, which demanded knowledgeable attention, gradually decayed, accelerated by shortage of garden labour after the war. In 1953 High Glanau passed to the Pike family, then to the Ward family and various owners who never stayed long. Presumably the large garden proved too much; the herbaceous borders were removed, the ribbon parterre planted with trees, a turquoise swimming pool was added on top of the grassway and the pergola lost its oak beams.

When the author bought the house in 2002, the herbaceous planting had gone, eight leylandii adorned the

octagonal pool, the wonderful stone plum pudding balls on the lower terrace and statues had been stolen and only Tipping's hard landscaping remained as the backbone of his romantic garden. With a little research, twenty-four photographic glass plates in the *Country Life* offices revealed, in clear black and white images, the house and garden in 1929 when Tipping wrote two articles about the house and the formal gardens, followed a week later by an article about the upper and lower woodland gardens. The *Country Life* articles describe specific work that he undertook in the garden, but also give valuable information about his way of gardening. He was candid about failures in his mixed borders planted in a naturalistic way. Now herbaceous planting with pronounced foliage or architectural interest in a border have become universal, but in Tipping's time this type of informal planting was novel. It has remained as standard in English gardens to the present day.

Over the next few years we removed the hedges on the terrace and the borders were reclaimed, backed by their warm grey sheltering walls. We learnt the vagaries of the hydraulic ram set in the stream 200 feet below the garden. So although there is no longer a pumped water supply to the house, there is ample water all day to pour through the leaden pump box into the old stone farm trough rimmed with ferns and into the basin below. John Blake Limited of Accrington in Lancashire were even able to supply Tipping's original invoice for the 'A' type Ram No. 12484 dated 1923. The water is then taken by underground pipe to the octagonal pool below the west side of the house. From there it progresses down the bank below to a wild pond frequented by great-crested newts, water snails and dragonflies. The journey is but half finished for the water has to descend a further 100 feet or more via various rills until it finally rejoins the stream from whence it originally came. The water features are an integral part

OPPOSITE Sam, the Whitehouses' Labrador, with family friends at High Glanau, c.1940.
LEFT Hugh Whitehouse on the statue of Bacchus in the upper woodland, c.1940.

191

of High Glanau, adding both sound and movement as well as enhancing the environment for the wildlife that is attracted to the garden. The frameyard was planted with fruit trees, with blocks of spring bulbs, primroses, cowslips, fritillaries, narcissi and camassias. A vegetable garden was made down the steep slope by making small wood-edged terraced beds, with fig, nectarine, morello cherry, pear and plum planted against the warm south-facing wall. In 2008 the swimming pool was removed so that Tipping's double herbaceous border running down to the pergola could be recreated using large drifts of irises, delphiniums, lupins, nepetas, achilleas and lilies. I keep the planting simple, remembering that Tipping had written, 'there is always the danger that an inventive mind will overcrowd the canvas'.

I find it is difficult to call High Glanau my garden. So much of Tipping's planning and planting has gone into its making and I have only pieced together its history. The garden itself has inspired me, as pillars and lost paths have reappeared, Tipping's original plants have been recognised and brilliant pink rhododendrons have burst into colour in May. But it is more than that; the anticipation as green shoots push through the soil, the heat given off the terrace walls, the spectacular view to the Brecon Beacons some forty miles away, the birdsong and bonfires, the scent of the wisteria, drifts of colour like a watercolour painting, the secret paths in the wood. Tipping created a secret world here and has left his mark in his own romantic way. We are lucky to be the custodians.

As Richard Haslam surmises,

Tipping had the good fortune to live when the historical study of domestic architecture tended towards the same ideal as did the practice of some of his architect contemporaries. His lifetime also coincided with what seems a golden age of gardening.

RIGHT The intrusive 1990s swimming pool removed and herbaceous borders recreated.

Conclusion

I F ONE TOOK only a cursory look at his life and work and the houses and gardens he created for himself, it might be possible to dismiss Henry Avray Tipping as inward-looking, limited to his own age and self-absorbed, as a man who used his great wealth to restore houses, create gardens, write and entertain simply for his own pleasure. This is not the truth. The legacy Tipping has left is massive and enduring. He has had a major influence on the history of taste, to the extent that he can reasonably be regarded as a seminal figure in the creation of the heritage culture and industry which are so important in Britain today.

First of all, Tipping has left a physical legacy, a substantial corpus of work which includes houses, newly created gardens and restored or redesigned gardens. As Christopher Hussey wrote of him,

> If he had left behind him only the series of gardens that he made for himself between 1888 and the present day, excluding those that he so much enjoyed laying out for his friends, he would have won for himself an honourable place among those who, during the past half-century, have given English gardening the leading place it occupies today in the garden art of the Western world.

His significance as a garden designer in the Arts and Crafts style has only been recognised in the last few years. Recent books on houses and gardens have made mention of him and have often used illustrations from the archives of *Country Life*, so that a new generation is now able to appreciate his combination of the formal and the natural and his ability to consider not only landscaping but planting.

ABOVE H. Avray Tipping drawn from memory by Christopher Hussey.

Secondly, and most importantly, Tipping was the most significant shaper of the style and contents of *Country Life*. What started off as just one more sporting publication came to give pride of place to historic houses and gardens (and, to a lesser extent, antique furniture). Through his choice of Christopher Hussey as his successor, this successful formula was continued and has been perpetuated into the present. Tipping was the great recorder of country houses, both through *Country Life* and through the subsequent magisterial books on houses and gardens which drew on his articles, and the impact of his work was made all the greater by the use of outstanding photographers. He was writing at that important period when the agricultural depression and then the Great War led to the decline of country houses; he recorded treasures that were to be lost and saved others. When there was a growing interest after the war for restoring castles, Tipping caught the enthusiasm with articles on Herstmonceux in Sussex, Saltwood and Leeds castles in Kent, and St Donat's in the Vale of Glamorgan. He also included articles on country house restorations, such as Dartington in Devon (where he advised on the garden), and Parham and the Messels' manor house at Nymans, both in Sussex. Ronald Tree's refurnishing at Kelmarsh in Northamptonshire and redecoration of Ditchley Park in Oxfordshire were all faithfully catalogued. *Country Life* also had articles on planning and preservation, the spoliation of the countryside, the destruction of historic buildings in towns and the threat to country houses through increased estate duty. In 1935, after Tipping's death, Lord Onslow acknowledged the influence of his writing for *Country Life*,

It has among other services rendered one in particular, namely, the description in minute detail of all the great country houses of England as they were actually lived in as the houses of their owners. Perhaps in twenty-five years' time none will exist in that condition.

Tipping even had an influence on the commercial side of the magazine. The introduction of death duties in 1894 had meant that large houses had either to be sold or let. Tipping often wrote articles on these houses before they were put up for sale in order to protect and, in some cases,

stop demolition of these great heirlooms; and eventually *Country Life* became the normal place to advertise such houses, hugely increasing the business of such firms as Knight, Frank and Rutley and at the same time increasing the advertising revenue of the magazine as rival estate agents vied for the most prestigious positions in its pages. Art and antique dealers also placed advertisements and saw the advantage of buying old houses to show off their stock. In fact Tipping was aware of the legacy he was leaving, as is revealed in his own words in the thousandth number of *Country Life* in 1916,

About 700 country houses of all styles and every size have been passed in review. But each one has been so treated as to show some merit, teach some lesson, and exercise some influence on the taste of today.

He added,

No wonder, then, that *Country Life* has become a document of great architectural importance....It is absolutely illuminating to the amateur, and gives hints and guidance to the many who propose to build or enlarge or alter or re-do their habitations and their gardens.

Thirdly, Tipping left a legacy through his wise choice of collaborators, with their superior knowledge of architecture, furniture and gardens, who went on to influence others. He was a generous mentor who saw potential talent and sought to bring out the best in those he guided. Most notable was Christopher Hussey, who was groomed for succession by Tipping from his teenage years and came to have much greater name recognition as a writer on architectural history – although in many ways he was simply continuing Tipping's work. Another protégé was Lawrence Weaver who introduced supplements championing the works of Edwin Lutyens and Robert Lorimer, thereby inspiring patrons to use them to build their new houses; and Tipping employed photographers Charles Latham and A.E. Henson and old furniture experts Margaret Jourdain and Percy Macquoid.

Macquoid, one of Tipping's oldest friends, joined *Country Life* in 1909 and the combination of his expertise and the benefits of good photography were heralded in an announcement in April 1911, 'so great is the present interest in the history of furniture' that the magazine 'will week by week present a picture of a piece of furniture so exactly catching its characteristics…that the very thing will appear to stand before us.' Long before the term 'networking' was ever used, Tipping was a master of the art. We can see this when Hudson chose Gertrude Jekyll to be Gardening Editor of *Country Life*. Tipping might have considered her as a rival because they were both experts in the design and planting of gardens; but his capacity for friendship and collaboration left no space for jealousy, even though her name, too, has outshone his own. Perhaps because of the breadth of his interests, perhaps because of his wealth, he was happy to see her take a wider stage for her very real gifts and encouraged her to welcome the talents of other collaborators. Thus in the pages she controlled we can find her retelling her experience at Munstead Wood, Tipping himself writing on Warley Place (1915) or Bodnant (1920) or the Chelsea Flower Show (1922), William Robinson describing his garden at Gravetye Manor and E.T. Cook, author of *The Century Book of Gardening* (March 1900), or E.H.M. Cox keeping readers abreast of the newest plants. More recently A.G.L. Hellyer, Lanning Roper and Christopher

Lloyd have also been important contributors. Tipping's direction and encouragement stand behind them all; and the photographs he commissioned of the plant-intensive formal gardens of the Edwardian era remain a great resource for garden historians.

In the long term, Tipping can be seen as the man behind the 'country living' idea, which caused wealthy people to aspire to own a country house and take an interest in their gardens. Leisured people of the eighteenth and nineteenth century may have had botany as a hobby, but Tipping, particularly through the articles which he wrote for *Country Life*, made practical gardening a respected leisure pursuit. The concept of 'country living' has developed in many ways and has reached all kinds of people: there was the garden city movement of which Tipping was a protagonist in Wales; visiting houses and gardens has become a popular activity (encouraged by organisations such as the National Trust and the National Gardens Scheme); Tipping's influence may even lie at the root of the country style in decoration and the endless country living magazines. It was through *Country Life* first of all that people, consciously or unconsciously, absorbed ideas seen in the photographs of a magazine and then repeated them in their own homes.

In all these ways Henry Avray Tipping has had a significant influence on the way we think about country living even today. He had a unique set of talents and knowledge: he was a historian whose work as a contributor for the *Dictionary of National Biography* gave him a deep knowledge of the great British families; he was an architect, concerned both with preserving old houses within the guidelines of the Society for the Protection of Ancient Buildings and also with building new houses; he had a social conscience which was expressed in his concern for garden villages and quality housing for working families; he was a practical gardener, with a confident knowledge and great experience of both landscaping and planting so that he was able to give realistic guidance to gardeners; he was a hugely industrious writer, now recognised as a key chronicler of houses and gardens, who quite consciously set out to teach others and to form taste. His money and his academic background gave him an entrée to many areas, so that he was widely consulted; and in turn, he was a go-between who introduced wealthy patrons to experts such as the people he had recruited for *Country Life*. He had many acquaintances and yet he was a private person, losing his family and never having one of his own, which seems to be why his importance has been largely forgotten and his influence so seriously underestimated.

Tipping was an enigma and an eccentric, a tireless worker and also a great scholar with a superb historical mind. His boundless energy for houses and gardens has influenced architectural historians, garden designers and interior designers throughout the twentieth century and into the twenty-first, so much so that he can be considered

the *éminence grise* behind those, like Hussey, who became more notable public figures. If we try to trace the source of the whole phenomenon of country living as a lifestyle choice, an ideal which persists to the present day, we will find a solitary figure sitting under a pergola in the lush Monmouthshire countryside: Henry Avray Tipping.

LEFT Tipping's dogs with Mathern Palace in the background in 1908.
BELOW The solitary seat in the pergola at Mounton, luxuriantly clothed with roses and so much admired by Gertrude Jekyll in *Garden Ornament* (photograph 1915).

Bitgisky. Cornwall

Bibliography

WORKS BY H. AVRAY TIPPING

BOOKS

In English Homes: The Internal Character Furniture & Adornments of some of the most Notable Houses of England Historically Depicted from Photographs Specially taken by C. Latham, 3 volumes, Country Life Ltd. and George Newnes, London, 1908–9.

Gardens Old and New: The Country House and its garden environment, volume 3, Country Life Ltd., London, 1908.

A Short History of Kensington Square, London, 1909.

Grinling Gibbons and the Woodwork of his age, Country Life Ltd., London, 1914.

The Story of the Royal Welsh Fusiliers, Country Life Ltd., London, 1915.

English Homes: Architecture from Medieval times to the early part of the nineteenth century, 9 volumes, Country Life Ltd., London, 1920–28.

> Period I – Vol. I: Norman and Plantagenet (1066–1485)
>
> Period II – Vol. I: Early Tudor (1485–1558)
>
> Periods I and II – Vol. II: Medieval and Early Tudor (1066–1558)
>
> Period III – Vol. I: Late Tudor and Early Stuart (1558–1649)
>
> Period III – Vol. II: Late Tudor and Early Stuart (1558–1649)
>
> Period IV – Vol. I: Late Stuart (1649–1714)
>
> Period IV – Vol. II: The Work of Sir John Vanburgh and his School (1699–1736 (co-authored with Christopher Hussey)
>
> Period V – Vol. I: Early Georgian (1714–60)
>
> Period VI – Vol. 1: Late Georgian (1760–1820)

English Furniture of the Cabriole Period, Jonathan Cape, London, 1922.

English Gardens, Country Life Ltd., London, 1925.

Old English Furniture: Its true value and function, Country Life Ltd., London, 1928.

The Late Marquis Curzon of Kedleston and H. Avray Tipping, *Tattershall Castle, Lincolnshire,* Jonathan Cape, London, 1929.

The Story of Montacute and its house, Country Life Ltd., London, 1933.

The Garden of To-day, Martin Hopkinson Ltd., London, 1933.

PLAYS

A Hibernian Hyperbole entitled The Three P's, or The Pig, The Paddy, and The Patriot M.P., C. Hooker, Westerham, performed at the Public Hall, Westerham, Kent, 1888.

The Imperious Maid: A comedy in three acts, G. Phillipson, Kingston-on-Thames, 1890.

SELECTED ARTICLES

'The Old Palace at Mathern and its Gardens 1', *The Garden,* 27 January 1900, pp.57–9.

'The Old Palace at Mathern and its Gardens 2', *The Garden,* 3 February 1900, pp.77–8.

'Two renovated cottages in Monmouthshire', *Country Life,* 21 March 1908, pp.411–13.

'Adcote, Shropshire', *Country Life,* 25 December 1909, pp.912–20.

'In the Garden', *Country Life,* 25 June 1910, pp.936–8.

'A Water Garden in the Natural Style', *Country Life,* 1 September 1910, p.364.

'Mathern Palace, Monmouthshire', *Country Life,* 19 November 1910, pp.718–25.

LEFT Watercolour by G.H. Kitchin of Portgisky, showing Jack Tremayne's converted boathouse and Tipping's holiday cottage above.

'The Yews, Windermere', *Country Life*, 18 May 1912, p.7* in supplement.

'The Country Homes of England as Revealed in a Thousand Numbers', *Country Life*, 4 March 1916, pp.300–8.

'The Gardens of Mounton House, Chepstow', *Country Life*, 28 July 1917, pp.84–91.

'Chequers I, Buckinghamshire', *Country Life*, 6 October 1917, pp.324–33.

'Chequers II, Buckinghamshire', *Country Life*, 13 October 1917, pp.348–55.

'Chequers III, Buckinghamshire', *Country Life*, 20 October 1917, pp.372–9.

'Percy Macquoid – an appreciation', *Country Life*, 28 March 1925, p.491.

'High Glanau I, Monmouthshire', *Country Life*, 8 June 1929, pp.822–9.

'High Glanau II, Monmouthshire', *Country Life*, 15 June 1929, pp.854–60.

'The Garden of Pleasure in England from Plantagenet to Victorian Times', *Journal of Royal Horticultural Society*, 1929, pp.260–71.

'English Garden Making under the Early Stuarts', *Journal of the Royal Horticultural Society*, 1930, pp.200–22.

'Gertrude Jekyll – an appreciation', *Country Life*, 17 December 1932, p.689.

BELOW A complete set of H. Avray Tipping's published books.

OTHER SOURCES

BOOKS AND CATALOGUES

Arts Council of Great Britain, 'Lutyens: The work of the English Architect Sir Edwin Lutyens', Exhibition Catalogue, Hayward Gallery, London, November 1981 – January 1982.

Aslet, Clive, *The Last Country Houses*, Yale, London and New Haven, 1982.

Attlee, Helena, *Charles Latham's Gardens of Italy*, Aurum Press, London, 2009.

Bradley-Hole, Kathryn, *Lost Gardens of England: From the archives of Country Life*, Aurum Press, London, 2004.

Bisgrove, Richard, *The Gardens of Gertrude Jekyll*, Frances Lincoln Ltd., London, 1992.

Bisgrove, Richard, *William Robinson: The Wild Gardener*, Frances Lincoln Ltd., London, 2008.

Blomfield, Reginald and F. Inigo Thomas, *The Formal Garden in England*, Waterstone, London, 1892.

Boyle, Eleanor Vere, *Days and Hours in a Garden*, Elliot Stock, London, 1892.

Brown, Jane, *Gardens of a Golden Afternoon*, Penguin, London, 1982.

Brown, Jane, *The English Garden Through the Twentieth Century*, Antique Collectors' Club, Woodbridge, 1999.

Clark, Alan, *A Good Innings: The Private Papers of Viscount Lee of Fareham*, John Murray, London, 1974.

Clifton-Taylor, Alec and A. S. Ireson, *English Stone Building*, Victor Gollancz, London, 1983.

Cook, E. T., *Gardening for Beginners*, Country Life Ltd., London, 1902.

Cornforth, John, *The Inspiration of the Past*, Viking, Harmondsworth, 1985.

Cornforth, John, *The Search for a Style*, Andrew Deutsch, London, 1988.

Cornforth, John, *London Interiors: From the archives of Country Life*, Aurum Press, London, 2000.

Darwin, Bernard, *Fifty Years of Country Life*, Country Life Ltd., London, 1947.

Edwards, Paul and Katherine Swift, *Pergolas, Arbours and Arches*, Barn Elms, London, 2001.

Elgood, George S. and Gertrude Jekyll, *Some English Gardens*, Longmans, Green & Co., London, 1904.

Elliott, Brent, *The Country House Garden: From the archives of Country Life*, Mitchell Beazley, London, 1995.

Festing, Sally, *Gertrude Jekyll*, Viking, London, 1991.

Gordon, Catherine, *Cotswold Arts and Crafts Architecture*, Phillimore & Co., Chichester, 2009.

Gradidge, Roderick, *Dream Houses*, Constable & Co. Ltd., London, 1980.

Guildford Borough Council, *Nature and Tradition, The Arts and Crafts Movement in Surrey*, Davey, John and John Flower (eds.), 1993.

Hall, Michael, *The English Country House: From the archives of Country Life 1897–1939*, Mitchell Beazley, London, 1994.

Head, Alice M., *It could never have happened*, William Heinemann Ltd., London, 1939.

Helmreich, Anne, *The English Garden and National Identity*, Cambridge University Press, Cambridge, 2002.

Hitchmough, Wendy, *Arts and Crafts Gardens*, V&A Publications, London, 2005.

Holroyd, Michael, *Lytton Strachey: A Biography*, Penguin, London, 1971.

Hussey, Christopher, *The Life of Sir Edwin Lutyens*, Country Life Ltd., London, 1950.

Jekyll, Gertrude and Edward Mawley, *Roses for English Gardens*, Country Life Ltd., London, 1902.

Jekyll, Gertrude, *Colour in the Flower Garden*, London, Country Life Ltd. and George Newnes, London, 1908.

Jekyll, Gertrude and Lawrence Weaver, *Gardens for Small Country Houses*, Country Life Ltd., London, 1912.

Jekyll, Gertrude and Christopher Hussey, *Garden Ornament*, Country Life Ltd., London, 1918.

Jenkins, J. Gilbert, *Chequers: A History of the Prime Minister's Buckinghamshire Home*, Pergammon Press, Oxford, 1967.

Leyland, John, *Gardens Old and New: The Country House and its garden environment*, volumes 1 and 2, Country Life Ltd., London, 1900 and 1903.

Major, Norma, *Chequers: The Prime Minister's Country House and its History*, HarperCollins, London, 1996.

Meyrick, Robert, *Things of Beauty: What two sisters did for Wales*, National Museum for Wales Books, Cardiff, 2007.

Musson, Jeremy, *The English Manor House*, Aurum Press, London, 1999.

Newman, John, *The Buildings of England: West Kent and the Weald*, Penguin, London, 1976.

Newman, John, *The Buildings of Wales: Gwent / Monmouthshire*, Penguin, London, 2000.

Ottewill, David, *The Edwardian Garden*, Yale University Press, London, 1989.

Reilly, C. H., *Scaffolding in the Sky*, George Routledge, London, 1938.

Richardson, Tim, *English Gardens in the Twentieth Century*, Aurum Press, London, 2005.

Ridley, Jane, *The Architect and His Wife: A Life of Edwin Lutyens*, Chatto & Windus, London, 2002.

Robinson, William, *The English Flower Garden and Home Grounds*, John Murray, London, first edition 1883, eleventh edition 1909.

Robinson, William, *Gravetye Manor, or Twenty Years' Work round an Old Manor House*, John Murray, London, 1911.

Sedding, John Dando, *Garden-Craft Old and New*, John Lane: The Bodley Head, London, 1891.

Snell, Reginald, *From the Bare Stem: Making Dorothy Elmhirst's Garden at Dartington Hall*, Devon Books, Exeter, 1989.

Spurling, Hilary, *Secrets of a Woman's Heart: The later life of Ivy Compton-Burnett 1920–1969*, Penguin, London, 1985.

Stamp, Gavin, *Edwin Lutyens Country Houses: From the Archives of Country Life*, Aurum Press, London, 2001.

Strong, Roy, *Country Life 1897–1997: The English Arcadia*, Country Life Ltd., London, 1997.

Tankard, Judith, *Gardens of the Arts and Crafts Movement*, Harry N. Abrams, New York, 2003.

Tankard, Judith and Michael Van Valkenburgh, *Gertrude Jekyll: A vision of Garden and Wood*, John Murray, New York, 1988.

Tankard, Judith and Martin A. Wood, *Gertrude Jekyll at Munstead Wood*, Bramley Books, Godalming, 1996.

Thorton, Lt Col L. H. and Pamela Fraser, *The Congreves*, John Murray, London, 1930.

Triggs, H. Inigo, *Formal Gardens in England and Scotland*, B.T. Batsford, London, 1902.

Wallinger, Rosamund, *Gertrude Jekyll's Lost Garden*, Antique Collectors' Club, Woodbridge, 2000.

Waterson, Merlin, *The Country House Remembered*, Routledge & Kegan Paul, London, 1985.

Watkin, David, *The Rise of Architectural History*, The Architectural Press, London, 1980.

Weaver, Lawrence, *English Leadwork: Its art and history*, B.T. Batsford, London, 1909.

Weaver, Lawrence, *The House and its Equipment*, Country Life Ltd., London, 1912.

Weaver, Lawrence, *Small Country Houses of To-day*, Country Life Ltd., London, 1912.

Weaver, Lawrence, *The Houses and Gardens of E. L. Lutyens*, Country Life Ltd., London, 1913.

Weaver, Lawrence, *The Country Life Book of Cottages*, Country Life Ltd., London, 1913.

Weaver, Lawrence, *Small Country Houses: Their repair and enlargement*, Country Life Ltd., London, 1914.

Whalley, Robin, *The Great Edwardian Gardens of Harold Peto*, Aurum Press, London, 2007.

Wilhide, Elizabeth, *Sir Edwin Lutyens: Designing in the English Tradition*, Pavilion Books, London, 2000.

Williams-Ellis, Clough, *Lawrence Weaver*, Geoffrey Bles, London, 1933.

Worsley, Giles, *England's Lost Houses: From the archives of Country Life*, Aurum Press, London, 2002.

Young, Michael, *The Elmhirsts of Dartington*, The Dartington Hall Trust, Totnes, 1996.

ARTICLES

Congreve, Lady, 'The Late H. Avray Tipping', *Country Life*, 25 November 1933, p.566.

Conway, Martin, 'Mounton House, Chepstow: The residence of Mr H. Avray Tipping', *Country Life*, 13 February 1915, pp.208–17.

Cornforth, John, 'The Husseys and the Picturesque' I, *Country Life*, 10 May 1979, pp.1438–41.

Cornforth, John, 'The Husseys and the Picturesque' II, *Country Life*, 17 May 1979, pp.1522–5.

Cornforth, John, 'Continuity and Progress – Christopher Hussey and Modern Architecture' I, *Country Life*, 22 October 1981, pp.1366–8.

Cornforth, John, 'Qualities of Generalship - Christopher Hussey and Modern Architecture' II, *Country Life*, 29 October 1981, pp.1468–70.

Cornforth, John, 'Balancing Past and Present: The Country House Between the Wars', *Country Life*, 8 January 1987, pp.80–4.

Cox, E. H. M., 'A Passing Generation: Gardening Trends and Pioneers of the Last Thirty Years', *Country Life*, 24 June 1939, p.667.

Edwards, Ralph, 'Percy Macquoid and Others', *Apollo*, May 1974, pp.332–9.

Girouard, Mark, 'Adcote, Shropshire', *Country Life*, 12 October 1970, pp.1056–9.

Haslam, Richard, 'Clytha Park I, Gwent', *Country Life*, 8 December 1977, pp.1718–21.

Haslam, Richard, 'Clytha Park II, Gwent', *Country Life*, 15 December 1977, pp.1826–9.

Haslam, Richard, 'The Houses of H. Avray Tipping I', *Country Life*, 6 December 1979, pp.2154–7.

Haslam, Richard, 'The Houses of H. Avray Tipping II', *Country Life*, 13 December 1979, pp.2270–3.

Hussey, Christopher, 'The Late H. Avray Tipping: Gardener and Antiquary', *Country Life*, 25 November 1933, p.567.

Hussey, Christopher, 'The Country Homes of England: A retrospect of 2,000 numbers of Country Life', *Country Life*, 18 May 1935, pp.516–22.

Hussey, Christopher, 'Edward Hudson: An appreciation', *Country Life*, 26 September 1936, pp.318–19.

Hussey, Christopher, 'Early Treatment of Country Houses', *Country Life*, 12 January 1967, pp.52–5.

Longville, Tim, 'Tipping's last project', *Country Life*, 30 September 2009, pp.48–53.

Maude, Pamela, 'Edward Hudson, the Founder of Country Life', *Country Life*, 12 January 1967, pp.58–60.

Roper, Lanning, 'The making of a great garden: Dartington Hall, Devon', *Country Life*, 6 July 1972, pp.6–9.

Singleton, H. G., 'H. Avray Tipping in Monmouthshire', *Severn and Wye Review*, volume 2 (1970–71), pp.43–7.

Singleton, H. G., 'A short history of Brasted Place and its owners', privately printed in 1954.

Spurling, Hilary, 'Few rivals and no superiors: Margaret Jourdain and Furniture History', *Country Life*, 14 June 1984, pp.1734–6.

Tankard, Judith B., 'Gardening with Country Life', *Hortus*, No. 30, Summer, 1994, pp.72–86.

Wheeler, David, 'A corner that is for ever England', *Country Life*, 16 July 1998, p.63.

Index

Author's acknowledgements

Many people made writing this book enjoyable and were wonderfully generous in lending photographs, diaries, watercolours and archives; sharing their knowledge and memories; showing me their homes and gardens and giving me lunches. I would particularly like to thank Lucinda Aldrich-Blake, Richard Astley, Tom and Penny Bailey, Jane Balfour, Francesa Bingham, John Borron, Susanna Bott, Barry Butler, Anto and Sarah Clay, Trish Collins, The Executors of the Estate of John Cornforth, Lord Crickhowell, Andrew Davies, Mary Dowling, Deborah Evans, Sarah Evans, Barbara Francis, Peter Garwood, Sir Richard Hanbury-Tenison, Brian Harwood, Hugh Holden, Andy Hopper, Peter Howell, Rosie Humphreys, Emma Jones, Andrew and Anne Langton, Penny Kift, Jean Mayne, Rodney Melville, Robert Meyrick, Graeme Moore, Jerrold Northrop Moore, John Newman, Neville and Juliet Purssell, David Ottewill, Anne Rainsbury, Mary Redvers, John Martin Robinson, John Ross, Sir Oliver and Lady Scott, Henry Slaughter, Judith Tankard, William Tansill, Paul Underwood, Tony Utting, David and Linda Whitehouse, Elizabeth Whittle, Robin Whalley and Dawson Williams. I am sincerely grateful to Cyril Hoare, who produced Tipping's diary for 1908 and so many of the personal photographs.

I am also indebted to Nancy McLaren for her encouragement and to Tim Mowl, Professor of History of Architecture & Designed Landscapes at the University of Bristol, for his belief that I could indeed write a book. Special thanks are due to Father Augustine Clark for help with editing and correcting, and Sue Porter Davison, Frances Marchant and Paul Groves for reading through the manuscript. Jane Crawley, my editor, was marvellously thorough, and Anne Wilson, the designer, managed to bring all my ideas to fruition. Justin Hobson of the Country Life Picture Library was endlessly patient. My thanks also go to the late Eric Wilkinson, doyen of the greenhouse and Helen Fergusson-Kelly, who kept the garden going while I wrote.

Lastly, thanks go to my family, my husband Hilary, and Georgina, Willoughby and Henry, who remained so supportive and enthusiastic throughout my quest for Tipping.

Picture credits